# *A Simple Guide to*
# Turning a Profit as a Contractor

By
## Melanie Hodgdon
and
## Leslie C. Shiner, MBA

# DEDICATION

This book is dedicated to our hard-working clients who sometimes need a little help. They entrust us with helping them make their businesses (and lives) better. It is a privilege to be partners in their success.

# ACKNOWLEDGEMENTS

The authors would like to express their thanks and appreciate to a number of people who were key players in the publication of this book.

To Shawn McCadden, CR, CLC, CAPS, Big 50 Remodeler, recipient of NARI's Harold Hammerman Spirit of Education Award, popular speaker, columnist, and consultant to remodelers nationwide, goes our heartfelt thanks for your many comments, edits, and contributions to the content. You tackled our first draft sitting in a deer blind during a frigid Maine November but were unable to add margin notes because your pen kept freezing. So you added the notes later. That's dedication. Your good-humored encouragement and enthusiasm for the book kept us going.

To Alan Hanbury, CGR, CAPS, CGP, speaker, past columnist for *Professional Remodeler* and other industry magazines, and treasurer of House of Hanbury Builders, Inc., you are the ultimate numbers guy and you kept us accurate and realistic. Thank you for your patience, concrete suggestions, and amazing turnaround.

To Michael Gorman, speaker, author, consultant, columnist, award-winning Big 50 and Top 500 remodeler, and principal of TechKnowledge, we took your comments and recommendations to heart, and the book is better for them.

To Sal Alfano, Editorial Director of Hanley Wood Business Media's Remodeling Group of magazines, websites, and newsletters – including *Remodeling, Replacement Contractor*, and *The Journal of Light Construction* – speaker, mentor, and former contractor, we wish to express our appreciation for the encouragement and insightful comments you provided. You graciously shared with us your years of experience writing and editing business and technical material for contractors to help us make this a book that people would actually want to read and be able to learn from.

To Mark Hooper of Angel Editing, thank you for your willingness to tackle the task of converting our many figures and graphics into print-worthy images when nobody else wanted to commit to the job. Responsibility for the body of the book looking as good and readable as it does is entirely due to your efforts. From the start, your enthusiasm, energy, and "can do" attitude (plus your amazing adherence to deadlines) has been a lifesaver.

# TABLE OF CONTENTS:

FOREWORD ................................................................................................1

PREFACE ....................................................................................................5

CHAPTER 1 – A SENSE OF DREAD ...........................................................8

Time to make a change............................................................................9

CHAPTER 2 – HOPE IS ON THE WAY.......................................................11

Pricing strategies.................................................................................12

First look at the financials ..................................................................13

Accrual vs. cash...................................................................................13

A look at cash flow..............................................................................14

CHAPTER 3 – YOUR NUMBERS ARE TALKING; ARE YOU

LISTENING? ..............................................................................................20

How overhead figures into pricing jobs.................................................22

Relating gross profit to your overhead requirements .............................23

Options for improving profit.................................................................24

Increase your volume...........................................................................24

Reports can show you what your slippage is .........................................25

Use numbers to run your business.........................................................26

CHAPTER 4 – MARKUP AND MARGIN MIX-UP.......................................28

Markup vs. margin...............................................................................29

Margin is a percentage of sales.............................................................30

Make numbers comparable ...................................................................31

Use historical information to create targets ...........................................33

Target net profit plus target overhead equals target gross profit...................34

Determine target sales volume ...............................................................35

Cost, overhead or profit – pick one!........................................................35

Different margins mean different target sales.........................................38

## CHAPTER 5 – SHOW ME THE MONEY! ...........................41

Estimating labor dollars ...........................................41

Hidden profit inside billing rates ............................42

Calculating margin based on gross wage ................42

Including the labor burden in the estimate ..............43

Jobs have labor, materials and subcontractor costs – what's the markup? .....44

Consider miscellaneous costs...................................45

## CHAPTER 6 – TOP OF THE CHARTS IT IS .....................48

Cost of Goods Sold....................................................48

Introduction to parallelism.......................................50

Value of parallelism – margin by cost type ..............51

Involving the whole team ..........................................52

## CHAPTER 7 – SHARING THE ENTHUSIASM ................53

Introducing changes..................................................53

Meeting resistance to change ....................................54

## CHAPTER 8 – ALL ABOARD!.......................................55

Willingness to change means understanding the change ................55

Involving the bookkeeper ..........................................56

Keep the team informed .............................................57

Procedural vs. mechanical changes ..........................58

## CHAPTER 9 – THE DEVIL IS IN THE DETAILS .............61

Involve the project manager .....................................61

Items/cost codes/phases are the backbone of job costing ...................62

Creating an estimate in a spreadsheet or in an accounting program............62

The project manager's role in your accounting software ...................63

Creating the right cost code list.................................64

Determine the level of detail that you need ...............64

Coming to an agreement ............................................65

Using the list as a checklist .......................................68

*Pick the items that are right for you and your needs* ...................................... 68

## CHAPTER 10 – ITEMIZE THIS! ...................................................... 71

*Everybody needs to agree on the list* ............................................... 71

*What are we tracking?* ...................................................................... 72

*Estimates will always have more detail than job costs* ................... 73

*Allow the list to grow over time, but with a plan* .......................... 76

*Create a list that works for each person as well as for the company* ............... 76

## CHAPTER 11 – I DON'T EVEN MAKE THAT MUCH .................... 78

*Look carefully at your extra employer costs* ................................... 78

*Start with the gross wage and add burdens* .................................... 79

*Workers' comp is also a burden attached to payroll* ....................... 80

*Liability insurance increases as payroll increases* .......................... 81

*Health insurance can be a significant burden* ................................ 83

*Consider all the burdens attached to an employee* ......................... 85

## CHAPTER 12 – THE SLUSH FUND ............................................... 88

*Look at the markup by cost type* ..................................................... 89

*Consider pricing on labor heavy jobs vs. subcontract heavy jobs* ................... 91

*Budget for labor hours as well as labor dollars* ............................. 92

## CHAPTER 13 – MORE DETAIL DOESN'T MEAN MORE INFORMATION ...................................................................................... 94

*Less detail can provide more useful reports* ................................... 95

*Separate items for different cost types* ........................................... 95

*Agree on definitions of items* ......................................................... 96

*Create a viable estimate for job costing* ......................................... 97

*An estimate worksheet needs to include tickler items* ................... 98

## CHAPTER 14 – AN IN-HOUSE REMODEL .................................. 102

*Markup formula revisited* ............................................................. 102

*When to make the switch* .............................................................. 104

*Moving forward with revisions* .................................................... 104

*Starting over considerations* ........................................................ *105*

*Every job may be different, but the estimating process isn't* ..................... *106*

*You can always changethe level of detail later* .............................. *107*

## CHAPTER 15 – TIME IS MONEY .......................................................... **109**

*The accuracy of a timecard is affected by when it is turned in* .................. *110*

*Consider daily timecards instead of weekly timecards* ........................... *111*

*Consider electronic solutions for gathering time data* ........................... *111*

*Make the timecard user-friendly* ................................................... *112*

*Use numeric codes (with description provided)* ................................... *114*

*Help everyone understand what tasks are included in each item* ............... *115*

*Make sure your timecard includes a signature line* .............................. *116*

*Include a notes section on your timecard* ........................................ *116*

## CHAPTER 16 –THEORY IS GOOD, PRACTICE MAKES PERFECT **119**

*Getting dependable results* ......................................................... *119*

*Creating a process – using a coding stamp* ....................................... *120*

*Testing the process* ................................................................ *121*

*Accurate coding takes teamwork* .................................................. *122*

*Job cost sooner rather than later* ................................................. *123*

*Learn more about the lead carpenter system* ...................................... *125*

*Accurate dating of bills mean accurate job costing* ............................. *126*

## CHAPTER 17 – BUY BUY CHAOS .......................................................... **128**

*It's easy to over order without a process* ......................................... *128*

*Implementing a purchase order system* ........................................... *129*

*Using your vendors to help job cost* ............................................... *130*

*Purchase orders can also be used for subcontract control* ...................... *131*

## CHAPTER 18 – TIMING IS EVERYTHING .................................................. **133**

*Figuring out your true profit* ...................................................... *133*

*Using a trended profit and loss statement* ........................................ *134*

*What causes fluctuating profits* ................................................... *134*

*Accrual basis statements are the way to go!* ...............................................135

*Profit based on invoicing can be misleading* ................................136

*Using the percent complete calculations for more accurate profit* ...............137

## CHAPTER 19 – WIP OR RIP ................................................................**140**

*Getting meaningful numbers* ......................................................140

*The WIP formula broken down into steps* ...................................141

*Determine your percent complete* ...............................................142

*Determine your actual earnings* .................................................142

*Determine if you are overbilled or underbilled* ............................143

*What if you are underbilled?* ....................................................144

*Adjust your P&L* .....................................................................145

## CHAPTER 20 – IF YOU DON'T ASK, YOU WON'T RECEIVE .......**148**

*What's in your invoice?* .............................................................148

*Have a standard policy for what invoices contain* ........................149

*How much information does the customer need to see?* ..................150

*Who's running the job?* .............................................................151

*What about time and materials invoicing?* ..................................151

*Providing T&M detail* ..............................................................152

*Try different templates to give you flexibility* ..............................153

## CHAPTER 21 – A LITTLE EXTRA HERE AND THERE, PLEASE ....**155**

*Using the right tools for financial management* ............................155

*Change orders will happen* ........................................................156

*Setting expectations for change orders* ........................................156

*Change orders add money and time* ............................................157

*When should change orders be paid for?* .....................................158

*What about on-the-fly changes?* .................................................159

*Forms and processes need to work together* .................................160

*Update your financial information with change orders* ..................162

## CHAPTER 22 – DON'T GET BURIED WITH PAPERWORK ...........**165**

Team buy-in on new procedures ................................................165

Reports have different levels of detail ........................................166

Different people need different reports .....................................167

Explore all available reports ....................................................167

Look at job cost reports ...........................................................169

Job cost reports can help you find slippage...............................169

Determine the "who" and "when" of reports...........................170

Cutting Mike loose ...................................................................171

EPILOGUE – SIX MONTHS LATER ..............................................174

Change for the better ...............................................................174

Hiding from problems never works ...........................................175

Using systems to stay out of trouble .........................................175

Reports can save you money and make you more profitable .........176

Using purchase orders can save you money................................177

Sticking to your guns ...............................................................178

Productivity can be measured ..................................................178

Keep valuable employees by being flexible.................................179

Think outside the box ..............................................................180

Growing with a lead carpenter system......................................180

Trusting the team .....................................................................181

APPENDIX A – GLOSSARY OF FINANCIAL AND ACCOUNTING
TERMS...................................................................................  183

APPENDIX B – SELECTED KEY CONCEPTS ...............................193

APPENDIX C – MARKUP TO MARGIN CONVERSION TABLE ....197

APPENDIX D – RESOURCES.....................................................198

ABOUT THE AUTHORS ...........................................................200

# FOREWORD

At a conference of remodelers in the mid-1990s, I presented a seminar on cost estimating. Having been a remodeler and custom-home builder myself for 20 years, I know how critical accurate estimating is to success in the construction business. I also know that the estimating process is tedious, and that talking about the process is even worse. The biggest challenge I faced that morning was holding the attention of an auditorium full of contractors anxious to go to lunch.

About midway through my 90-minute talk, I got to the part about marking up estimated costs to find the selling price. I explained that most contractors simply add "1" to their target margin and multiply. In other words, they assume that multiplying costs by 1.33 will earn them a 33% margin. I explained why that wouldn't work and would cause a loss on every job. I also made it clear why the estimating software on the market at the time offered no protection: all of the software used that same formula.

Abruptly, about a dozen people rose from their seats and headed for the doors. What had I said that was so offensive that it would drive people from the room? I began to worry if the next thing I said would cause a stampede for the doors.

My fears were unfounded. In the next few minutes, one by one, the contractors who had left filtered back into the room. After the session ended, one of them came up to the podium to tell me that he and the others had gone out into the hall to call their office managers and tell them not to send out any estimates until the company owner returned from the conference. Every one of them had pending bids that used a selling price based on the faulty formula that I had mentioned.

1

Here's the interesting part: I could give the same talk today, 15 years later, and half the audience would still discover that they are using the wrong formula to find the selling price for their jobs.

It has nothing to do with intelligence. Builders and remodelers are a smart bunch. They work with numbers and angles all day long, visualize how lines on paper translate into three-dimensional objects, track down unknown sources of leaks, drafts, weird smells, and other building maladies, and find ingenious solutions to nearly every construction problem they encounter.

And yet, when it comes to understanding revenue and expenses, markups and margins, overhead and profit, most contractors are in way over their heads. Why is that?

The reason, I think, is that most contractors end up in business by accident. They are attracted by the craft and achieve mastery through curiosity, diligence, and plain hard work. But nothing about learning the craft of construction prepares you for learning the business side.

Early on, the business model is simple: analyze the job, do the work, collect payment for the hours spent, repeat for the next job. Ironically, the better a craftsman gets at this simple model, the more demand there is for his services and the faster things become complicated. Some of the increased demand comes from customers with larger projects in mind who start asking how much the work will cost, so now the contractor must spend time estimating. He does this after hours, of course, because his days are still spent doing the work on site. Some projects take longer and can't be completed before the next job has to start, so the contractor hires an employee or two to help get the work done. Soon the craft is left far behind as the harried contractor spends his daylight hours hopping from site to site, supervising employees and subcontractors and solving problems. In between, he chases down missing special order materials at the lumberyard, spars with building officials at the permit office, and meets with prospective customers to generate new work. This leads to more time spent estimating – now also on weekends as well as evenings. All of this escalating activity makes it even more critical to keep costs for one job from mingling with costs for another and to isolate construction costs from other business expenses.

Some contractors never adjust to this rapidly changing state of affairs;

others consider the increasing burden of what they call "paperwork" to be a necessary evil; still others hire a bookkeeper and assume that the problem is solved. But even those who are motivated to educate themselves find that there are very few resources available.

Fortunately, one excellent resource has just been added, and it is the book you are holding. There are any number of bookkeeping how-to manuals on the market, plenty of accounting texts, and lots of books on managing a small business. Most of them, however, are written by bookkeepers and accountants for bookkeeping and accounting students. Very few focus on the business of construction and remodeling.

This book does. I have known both authors for quite a few years. The advantage they bring to their work is not merely their understanding of the unique issues construction company owners face, but their understanding that a contractor is not a bookkeeper and never will be. Both authors have worked with building and remodeling contractors for so many years that they know about their control issues, their optimism, their tendency to make decisions based on a gut feeling, and perhaps most importantly, their dread of paperwork.

This comes through in the book's narrative approach. The last thing a contractor wants to do is read a set of dull instructions on how to set up his books. But contractors love a good story, and that's what they get from the moment they are introduced to Mike, Marcie, and Frankie, of Best Builders Ever, and its aptly named consultant, Hope. The narrative format personalizes and humanizes all of the abstract concepts that non-accountants find so intimidating.

Make no mistake: This is a business text. But it reads more like a mystery. All of the basics are covered, including cash flow analysis, distinguishing job costs from overhead expenses, and calculating markup. But each piece of the puzzle is introduced as part of a scenario that will resonate with readers. Most contractors will recognize themselves immediately in the expertly imagined scenario the authors create for their fictional construction company. The way the events unfold, the interaction of the characters, and, most especially, the internal thought processes of the fictitious owner of Best Builders Ever feel completely real and familiar.

It will also raise their business IQ, and that's the point. If keeping the books, tracking job costs, pricing estimates, and figuring out whether you made any money or not have always been a mystery to you, then you've come to the right place.

I'm sure that any contractor who needs this book and is lucky enough to find it will be interrupted in his reading more than once by an irresistible urge to overhaul his business. As necessary and inevitable as that overhaul is, I strongly suggest reading all the way to the end and working through the examples before changing anything. But, knowing contractors as I do, they will probably, like those contractors who left in the middle of my estimating seminar all those years ago, leap to their feet at the end of each chapter and dash off to change whatever it is that they were just reading about.

Fortunately for them, the mystery of Best Builders Ever is so engaging that it will draw them back again and again to find out what happens next. And they just might end up saving their business…in spite of themselves.

Sal Alfano
Editorial Director
Hanley Wood Business Media's Remodeling Group
Washington, D.C.

# PREFACE

## WHY BUY THIS BOOK?

The first time you picked up a hammer, were you thinking about remodeling a house or running a construction company? Most contractors came up through the ranks. You probably know an awful lot about building a project but very little about building a company.

This is the book you should have bought the day you decided you could make more money running a construction company than banging nails for somebody else. It provides you with the answers to those business questions that plague contractors: what am I doing wrong and what's stopping me from making the money I deserve? Whether you're a custom home builder, remodeler, or subcontractor, this book will help you navigate the business ownership maze.

You'll meet Mike, owner of Best Builders Ever, a remodeler who is working too hard and not making enough. An unexpected event awakens him to the flaws in his company's systems, and he's forced to re-evaluate how he conducts business.

Best Builders Ever may be a company just like yours, and some of Mike's struggles may feel familiar. And that's no accident, because Best Builders Ever illustrates the most common errors the authors have experienced in a combined 40+ years of consulting. Using Mike's company as the focus, this book will take you through the process of identifying and correcting common flaws in office and production systems. The result is that Mike gets the tools he needs so that he can run his business more profitably by:

- Understanding his true cost of labor for better pricing and labor management

- Doing cost-based estimating for improved analysis

- Pricing jobs to cover all his costs and obtain a target profit

- Getting accurate and timely job cost reports so he can manage jobs from start to finish

- Producing meaningful financial statements that can be used to help him make good financial decisions

Along the way, Mike will face and overcome those challenges typical of small business owners trying to understand their numbers, adopt new systems, and create a repeatable process for profit.

## HOW IS THIS BOOK DIFFERENT?

Although numerous books have been written about business management, this book is different in two ways. First, it is specific to the small to mid-sized builder or remodeler. Second, while it does contain financial theory, it is written in easy-to-understand, plain English.

This is not a "how to" book, but a "what and why" book. This book is intended for owners and managers because they are the ones who need to understand the business practices described. All too often, in the authors' experience, owners try to delegate away financial responsibilities to office managers, bookkeepers, tax accountants, or their spouses. This is the book that helps owners learn what they need to know in order to evolve from being *contractors* to *business owners* who deliver the service of building or remodeling.

After years of listening to clients and seminar attendees clamor for a simple, understandable financial and business management manual for contractors, the authors decided it was time to meet that need. This book aims to teach builders or remodelers how to improve internal systems, run their books, and obtain valid and reliable financial and job cost reports from which they can make good management decisions. It provides specific solutions to common construction business financial challenges.

# HOW SHOULD I USE THIS BOOK?

The authors recommend that readers start at Chapter 1 and read straight through, since the concepts presented in this book build upon each other. However, some readers may choose to pick chapters at random, or to work directly from the numerous charts, formulas, and equations within the body of the book. In addition, readers can use the book as a reference because key formulas, equations, terms, and concepts are found in the appendix.

# IS THIS BOOK APPLICABLE TO ANY FINANCIAL SOFTWARE PACKAGE?

While Mike's company uses QuickBooks, this book is not limited to companies that use QuickBooks. The examples used and the result shown can be achieved in any small business software. This book is *not* a click-by-click book on how to use QuickBooks. The authors believe that combining financial management theory and solutions with instructions on how to use QuickBooks would result in a thick, intimidating book. They also felt that information on management would be more appropriate to owners and managers, while books on how to actually implement financial systems using QuickBooks software would be more appropriate to those personnel responsible for setting up, entering data into, and producing reports from the software. Therefore, for more "how to" answers specific to QuickBooks, check other books in the *Money Maze* series.

# CHAPTER 1 – A SENSE OF DREAD

You know how some days you wake up with a sense of dread? Mike woke up feeling uncomfortable. He knew he had a lot to do that day, but as he drove to the office, he was overcome by a sense of impending doom. He brushed it aside, and as he walked into the office, he was greeted by Marci, his sometimes-dour bookkeeper. But today, Marci was in a great mood. She greeted him with a big smile and handed him a pink message slip. On it were the words: "WE GOT THE JOB!"

Mike was thrilled. He'd been courting this customer for months, which seemed like years. He'd almost given up when Marci told him that the Wileys had just called and they wanted to go ahead with the job. This was the biggest job that Mike had ever landed, and for a few minutes he was on cloud nine!

Then the doubts started creeping in. Would he have enough cash to run the job? Did he have enough field staff? Had he sold it for a high enough price to cover all his costs – costs that had risen dramatically since he'd originally priced the job? He brushed aside those concerns. Things had always worked out in the past, and because the job was so big, he was sure there was a lot of profit in it. He was also excited because now he didn't have to spend so much energy selling work for a while. He wanted to call his project manager to share the good news.

As Mike picked up the phone to call Frankie, he noticed a package on his desk. It was from his CPA, and it was very thick. Then Mike realized that it was March 8th and his corporate tax return was due in one week. He opened the package and the dread he'd felt when he woke up that morning returned.

His tax return showed that even though he'd been making regular estimated tax payments, he still owed $12,000. He immediately called out to Marci and asked how much money was in the bank. As Mike impatiently waited for Marci to open up her QuickBooks file, he drummed his fingers on his desk. He wished he could get this information without having to ask Marci. He hated to feel dependent on her, and Mike suspected that she enjoyed the power she held: she didn't want anybody else messing up QuickBooks. Frankie said she had an 'attitude' and if she was out sick on payday, nobody got paid! At first he'd been appreciative that she'd taken over all the bookkeeping, but now he was starting to feel uneasy that he couldn't figure out what was going on by himself.

Several minutes later, Marci yelled across the office. "I haven't entered all the checks from yesterday, but so far we have about $3,000 in the account." Panic set in; how did Mike get in this situation? He was about to start the biggest job of his life and there wasn't even enough money to pay the taxes.

With a deep sigh, Mike reluctantly called Marci into his office. He'd decided to see where he was on the three jobs he was finishing. He knew in his head he was over budget on one of them, but he was sure there was enough money in the others to cover it. "Can you print me out the job cost reports for the three jobs we're finishing? I need to know how much money we've spent on each one so far."

Marci stood there with a blank look on her face. "Job cost reports? I don't have our spreadsheets up to date. I can work on them and come up with some numbers in a few days. It depends on how much information I can get from Frankie."

Mike called Frankie, his project manager. He knew Frankie could help. He asked Frankie how much money was left in the budget for the jobs he was working on. Frankie told him to ask Marci.

## TIME TO MAKE A CHANGE

Mike slumped in his chair. What a mess! Mike thought he'd built a good remodeling company, but now he wasn't sure. The additional taxes were a surprise. Discovering there wasn't enough cash in the bank was a surprise. Realizing that he'd have to wait a few days just to find out how things stood with the three current jobs was a surprise. The day had been filled with surprises, and only one of them – getting the Wiley job – was good.

What should he do?

He took a deep breath and decided he should spend the next hour making a plan. Who could he call? Who could help?

He'd hired consultants before, but he never liked them and they just seemed to waste his money. They talked in generalities or seemed unaware of the special challenges he faced as a remodeler. But he remembered that when he was playing poker last weekend, his remodeler buddy, George, had told him about the consultant he'd hired who had whipped his company into shape. George was glowing about this woman who really understood their industry. George couldn't say enough about having made the commitment to understand his numbers and how much having a handle on his financials had reduced his stress level. George had even said something about using his accounting software as a management tool to help him run his business and give him back his life.

Mike thought about it. What did he have to lose? He was already in financial trouble; now he was starting to wonder whether there were other things about his business that were in similar shape. He knew that staying on the same course wouldn't solve his problems. He picked up the phone and called George to get this woman's phone number. This time, he was going to do it right!

### What Mike learned:

1. *Things may feel fine right up until you run out of cash.*

2. *You may not miss job cost reports until you need them and don't have them.*

3. *Businesses can be managed by the numbers.*

### Self-assessment questions:

1. *How readily available to you is critical financial and job costing information?*

2. *Have you ever been surprised by information provided by your accountant?*

3. *When you sell a job, are you consistently confident about how you've priced it?*

# CHAPTER 2 – HOPE IS ON THE WAY

Mike had to wait a few days for an appointment with this consultant, and he was anxious to start working with her. He knew little about her, except that his friend, poker buddy, and fellow contractor, George, had said that she'd changed his life. So, before she arrived, Mike checked out her website.

He learned that Hope specialized in the construction industry and the majority of her glowing recommendations came from contractors. He even knew several of them. One sentence in her company description stood out. "I have found that many contractors are stuck in a cycle of growing out of control and shrinking back to try to gain control and are always looking for that magic size." That described him! Then he went to on to see that her Mission Statement was just what he was looking for:

> *My mission is to help contractors learn how to manage company resources effectively, measure and control costs, and to create financial and strategic plans to maximize profits regardless of the size of the business. With these things in place, owners can run their companies with greater efficiency, profitability, and satisfaction. This in turn helps them create a better life-work balance.*

She agreed to meet with Mike at 10:00 on Friday. As that time approached, he considered the irony of her name, Hope. He certainly had hope that she'd help him!

As Hope walked in the door, Mike was struck by her confident demeanor. But he'd been fooled by consultants before. How could this woman really understand the problems he faced if she wasn't a contractor herself? And she was a woman! Mike had only scheduled two hours with her, and if she couldn't provide any valuable information in that time, she was "outta here!"

11

Mike explained to Hope that he needed to find a way to get better handle on his jobs, like George had done. He told her that he couldn't seem to get any good job cost reports. He said to Hope, "I'm concerned that this new job, the Wiley job, is very big. While this makes it potentially very profitable, it could also produce a large loss."

## PRICING STRATEGIES

As they settled into Mike's office, Hope began, "Mike, let's examine your pricing strategy. Tell me a little bit about how you price a job. Which is more important to you: coming up with a price that you're confident will lead to a sale or coming up with a price that you know will cover your costs and produce a target profit?"

Unaccustomed to explaining his pricing "strategy" to another person, Mike was momentarily stuck for an answer. "Well," he said hesitantly, "I don't see much point in coming up with a contract price that I don't believe the customer will go for. So naturally I start out with the markup I'd like to get, but if the price looks too high, maybe once in a while I'll play with lowering the markup until I get something that I'm confident will sell.

"For example," he continued, "I've created a budget for the Wiley job and marked it up with 15% overhead and 10% profit. I've read all the articles that said that the 10% overhead and 10% profit was never enough, and so I figured I'd charge more. I've heard that some people were marking up their jobs 35% or more, but I really wanted this job and I wasn't sure I could get it if I charged so much. So, I compromised with this markup and figured it would be OK."

"Hmmm," said Hope. "And has that pricing structure paid off for you on your past jobs? Do you feel things are going pretty well for the company financially?"

A week ago, Mike would have answered such a question with a confident "You bet!" but now he just wasn't so sure. "I guess I *thought* things were in pretty good shape, but if I didn't have some doubts right now, you wouldn't be here." Mike smiled to remove any possible sting from the remark.

# FIRST LOOK AT THE FINANCIALS

After hearing Mike's take on things, Hope asked if she could see Mike's Profit and Loss (P&L) Statement and his previous year's tax return. She sat down at Marci's computer and printed out some reports. Then she asked if she could have 30 minutes to analyze, review and revise the reports to be able to better show Mike what she could do for him. He said sure with a hint of a smile – this would be where the rubber hit the road and he'd see if Hope really knew her stuff.

Hope worked quietly on the computer for the next 25 minutes. After printing out a few reports, she told Mike she was ready to meet with him again. Hope showed Mike his Profit and Loss Statement. Her first comment shocked Mike. "Did you know that you lost more than $80,000 last year?"

Mike said, "That can't be right! I just found out that I owe the IRS $12,000!"

# ACCRUAL VS. CASH

Hope explained that the tax return was prepared on a cash basis – meaning that he'd taken in about $42,000 more in cash last year than he'd paid out for expenses. But for her analysis, she'd looked at the P&L on an *accrual basis*, based on when the income was actually invoiced and the expenses incurred. "Many contractors look at their financial statements on a cash basis. This means that you show income when you deposit a check from a client, and you show expenses when you pay a check to a vendor or subcontractor. The problem with cash-basis reports is that they can be very misleading. In fact, they may make you look more profitable than you really are. If you don't have the cash to pay the bills, then you don't even see the costs. Actually most cash-basis companies look like they are breaking even right up to the point that they have to close their doors and go out of business!

"I suggest that we look at your financials on an accrual basis. This means that whether or not you've actually paid a bill, as long as it's entered, you'll see it as a cost on your financials. And whether or not your customer has actually paid you, if you've created an invoice, it will show up as income. This allows you to get a better picture of what you owe

13

others compared with what others owe you on a daily basis. Therefore, it is better to look at your financials on an accrual basis to be able to determine profitability."

Since Mike had had a taxable cash profit and an accrual loss, she suspected one reason. She turned to Mike and asked, "Did you have a few jobs that started in November or December?"

Mike realized that that was just about the time these last three jobs started. How did Hope know that? He answered, "Yes, but I don't understand what that has to do with anything."

Hope explained one reason why he could have a cash profit and accrual loss. "When there's a delay between when you receive payments from your customers and when you actually pay your subs and suppliers, this produces a cash profit. For example, if you receive cash from the customer in December for the cabinets, but don't pay for the cabinets until January, you appear profitable on a cash basis. But if you show both the income and the expense of those cabinets in December, which happens when you look at the report on an accrual basis, your profit is significantly reduced."

## A LOOK AT CASH FLOW

Hope continued, "We're going to look at accrual-based accounting later, but for now let's focus on cash flow. Cash flow is usually best when jobs are about 20-50% done. First, you're often still on or under budget and the customer is still paying regularly, so your jobs appear to be profitable. Secondly, if the invoices are front loaded, you can be what's called 'cash ahead' of the customer or overbilled. The customer is paying for work before you have to pay for it. It's not until the job is nearing the end that the cash flow crunch really hits. You've already invoiced the customer for most of the money, yet you still have to come up with additional cash to finish the job. And if the job is not on budget, the costs at the end are much more than anticipated."

Hope explained, "Let's look at a sample job to see how the cash flows on a weekly basis.

"If we start with a job that costs $31,000 and sells for $42,000 and you bring the job in on budget, you should earn $11,000 to cover overhead and make a profit. To calculate your gross margin, simply take your gross profit in dollars and divide by the sales price." (Refer Figure 2-1.)

| Sales price | - | Job Costs | = | Gross Profit |
|---|---|---|---|---|
| $42,000 | | $31,000 | | $11,000 |
| | | | | |
| Gross Profit | ÷ | Sales price | = | Gross Margin |
| $11,000 | | $42,000 | | 26% |

**Figure 2-1. To determine gross profit, subtract job costs from the sales price. To determine gross margin, divide gross profit in dollars by the sale price of the job.**

Hope continued, "It's impossible to attribute overhead costs to individual jobs – after all, how could you assign office rent to a specific job? But *on average*, each job must be priced to cover its fair share of annual overhead and to produce its fair share of profit. For this example, let's assume that you have determined that your overhead last year was 19% of your last year's revenue. Therefore, this job would have to cover approximately $8,000 of overhead ($42,000 x 19% = $8,000). So that needs to be subtracted from the gross profit to determine your net profit. This tells us that you should have a net profit of $3,000, or a net profit margin of 7%. (Refer Figure 2-2.)

| Gross Profit | - Job's share of overhead | = | Net Profit |
|---|---|---|---|
| $11,000 | $8,000 | | $3,000 |
| | | | |
| Net profit | ÷ | Selling price = | Net Profit Margin |
| $3,000 | | $42,000 | 7% |

**Figure 2-2. To determine net profit, subtract overhead costs from gross profit. To determine net profit margin, divide the net profit in dollars by the selling price.**

"If we were to rearrange this information as it would appear in a Profit and Loss for just this job, it would look like this." (Refer Figure 2-3.)

| | | Margin |
|---|---|---|
| Income | $42,000 | |
| Cost of Goods Sold | -$31,000 | |
| Gross Profit | $11,000 | 26% |
| | | |
| Overhead | -$8,000 | |
| Net Profit | $3,000 | 7% |

**Figure 2-3. Sample job as displayed in a P&L**

Hope asked Mike if the numbers seemed likely. Mike said that if he could consistently achieve 26% gross margin and 7% net profit margin, he'd be OK with that.

Next, Hope showed him a cash flow spreadsheet. (Refer Figure 2-4.) "Now let's look at how the cash flows throughout the job. Assume that the job lasted 10 weeks. Notice the last column that shows how the net cash changes each week."

| Week # | Cash Out | | | Cash In | | Net Weekly | Cumulative |
|---|---|---|---|---|---|---|---|
| | Job Cost | Overhead | Cumulative | Payments | Cumulative | Cash | Net Cash |
| 1 | $3,500 | $800 | $4,300 | $7,500 | $7,500 | $3,200 | $3,200 |
| 2 | $2,500 | $800 | $7,600 | | $7,500 | -$3,300 | -$100 |
| 3 | $2,000 | $800 | $10,400 | $7,500 | $15,000 | $4,700 | $4,600 |
| 4 | $3,000 | $800 | $14,200 | | $15,000 | -$3,800 | $800 |
| 5 | $4,500 | $800 | $19,500 | $7,500 | $22,500 | $2,200 | $3,000 |
| 6 | $5,000 | $800 | $25,300 | | $22,500 | -$5,800 | -$2,800 |
| 7 | $4,000 | $800 | $30,100 | $7,500 | $30,000 | $2,700 | -$100 |
| 8 | $2,000 | $800 | $32,900 | | $30,000 | -$2,800 | -$2,900 |
| 9 | $3,500 | $800 | $37,200 | $7,500 | $37,500 | $3,200 | $300 |
| 10 | $1,000 | $800 | $39,000 | $4,500 | $42,000 | $2,700 | $3,000 |
| Totals | $31,000 | $8,000 | | $42,000 | | | |

**Figure 2-4. Cash flow for a 10-week period. Net weekly cash is generated by subtracting job costs and overhead from payments.**

Mike considered the numbers. He could see that over the course of ten weeks, there were job costs each week, although the amount fluctuated. He also noticed that overhead was steady each week at $800. However, the cash came in larger amounts less frequently, so it was a little hard to see how cash and costs were tracking. "I see what you're getting at," Mike said, "but it's hard to really tell what's happening just from the chart. I see there are some weeks I'm up and some I'm down, but it seems to work out in the end."

"That's a great observation, Mike," noted Hope. "It's really hard to see trends from a chart full of data. However, if we graph the data, things become easier to interpret." Then Hope drew a simple graph of the data in the chart. (Refer Figure 2-5.)

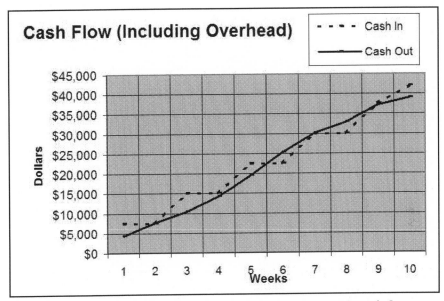

**Figure 2-5. Graph showing cash in and cash out over ten-week period.**

"Notice that even though this job produced a profit (after overhead) the cash flow changed about halfway through the job. The line representing 'cash in' was higher than the line representing 'cash out' during the first half of the job, while the job was ramping up. When it was in full swing, the tides turned and the job was cash poor until the final payment."

Mike agreed that the chart was easier to read, but observed, "The lines look pretty close, though, and the 'cash in' line is higher again by the end of the job."

Hope smiled and said, "Yes, they do look close on this graph. But now, let's see how things look when you look at the net cash each week." (Refer Figure 2-6.)

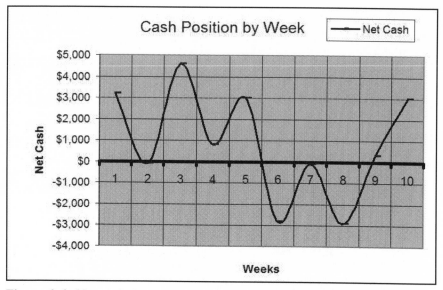

**Figure 2-6. Net cash by week for a ten-week period showing that early deposits and late costs can create cash flow crunches during the second half of the job.**

With the net cash so obviously dropping during the second half of the job, Mike could really see what Hope meant. When he thought about his three current jobs, which all started right after Thanksgiving, he realized that Hope was right – back at the end of December, around the fifth week, he was in a good cash position, just like the graph. Now it was March, those jobs were finishing up, and he was running out of cash. This made sense! Just by looking at the chart and seeing that at the end of the year, he was up in cash, now he understood why he had to pay so much in taxes. Even though he'd repeatedly asked his accountant about this, he never got a straight answer. This was the first time anyone had ever explained it in a way he could understand. Maybe Hope really did know her stuff.

***What Mike learned:***

1. *Your business may look one way on a tax return (reported on a cash basis) and a very different way from "inside" (management reports on accrual basis).*

2. *There are identifiable reasons for why a company runs out of cash.*

3. *If running out of cash is explainable, it may also be avoidable.*

4. *It's critical to arrange data so it is meaningful to you.*

5. *His accountant may be an excellent resource for getting his taxes filed, but not for getting business management advice.*

## Self-assessment questions:

1. *Are you reading reports using the same basis (cash vs. accrual) on which your tax return is created and do you understand the difference?*

2. *Do you try to sell work by price rather than value?*

3. *Do you try to sell work on gut vs. fact?*

4. *Do you front-load your customer payment schedule or do you finance jobs for your customers?*

5. *Do you ever use deposit money on a job that hasn't started in order to pay costs on other ongoing jobs?*

6. *Do you know whether or not your jobs are on budget as they're being produced?*

# CHAPTER 3 – YOUR NUMBERS ARE TALKING; ARE YOU LISTENING?

Hope then showed Mike his Profit and Loss Statement (P&L) for last year on an accrual basis. He'd seen this before, but it really never made sense. Hope said, "The way this is set up is not helping you. You need to track your job costs separately from your overhead costs." She then showed him a spreadsheet that contained the same information but was set up differently, and they looked at the two side by side. (Refer Figure 3-1.) She pointed out that the bottom lines of both P&L's were the same, but she'd reorganized the information to make the report more useful.

### Mike's Original P&L

| | |
|---|---:|
| **Income** | |
| Construction revenue | $800,000 |
| Interest income | -$58 |
| Total Income | $799,942 |
| | |
| **Overhead Expense** | |
| Advertising/promotion/marketing | $1,840 |
| Bank and finance charges | $32 |
| Depreciation expense | $2,800 |
| Insurance - general | $7,520 |
| Interest expense | $2,400 |
| *Licenses and permits* | $14,945 |
| *Materials* | $208,791 |
| Miscellaneous | $598 |
| Office supplies | $8,571 |
| *Payroll Expenses* | $341,368 |
| Penalties and fines | $1,760 |
| Professional fees | $11,920 |
| Rent | $17,600 |
| *Small tools, maintenance & repair* | $15,462 |
| *Subcontractors* | $218,411 |
| Taxes & licenses | $1,600 |
| Telephone | $4,800 |
| Travel & entertainment | $1,848 |
| Utilities | $3,720 |
| Vehicle costs | $14,744 |
| Total Overhead Expenses | $880,731 |
| | |
| **Net Profit from Operations** | -$80,789 |
| Net Profit Margin | -10.1% |

### Hope's Revised P&L

| | |
|---|---:|
| **Income** | |
| Construction revenue | $800,000 |
| **Total Income** | **$800,000** |
| | |
| **Cost of Goods Sold** | |
| *Materials* | $208,791 |
| *Production labor - gross wages* | $175,573 |
| *Payroll Taxes and Burdens* | $61,451 |
| *Subcontractors* | $218,411 |
| *Permits* | $14,300 |
| *Small tools & equipment* | $7,731 |
| **Total Cost of Goods Sold** | **$686,257** |
| | |
| **Gross Profit** | **$113,743** |
| **Gross Profit Margin** | **14.2%** |
| | |
| **Overhead Expense** | |
| Advertising/promotion/marketing | $1,840 |
| Bank and finance charges | $32 |
| Depreciation expense | $2,800 |
| Insurance - general | $7,520 |
| Interest expense | $2,458 |
| Licenses & non-job permits | $645 |
| Maintenance & repair (not vehicle) | $7,731 |
| Miscellaneous | $598 |
| Office supplies | $8,571 |
| Office and admin-salaries | $38,400 |
| Office and admin-burden | $10,944 |
| Officer/owner-salaries | $55,000 |
| Penalties and fines | $1,760 |
| Professional fees | $11,920 |
| Rent (or mortgage interest) | $17,600 |
| Taxes & licenses | $1,600 |
| Telephone | $4,800 |
| Travel & entertainment | $1,848 |
| Utilities | $3,720 |
| Vehicle costs | $14,744 |
| **Total Overhead Expenses** | **$194,531** |
| **Overhead as % of Income** | **24.2%** |
| | |
| **Net Profit from Operations** | **-$80,789** |
| **Net Profit Margin** | **-10.1%** |

**Figure 3-1. Mike's original P&L did not separate job-related costs from overhead costs. Hope's revised version separates job-related costs (Cost of Goods Sold accounts) from overhead costs (Expense accounts) for better analysis. Accounts that have been rearranged are shown in italics. "Payroll Expense" has been split between wages and payroll taxes paid to production workers and wages and payroll taxes paid to overhead (office) workers. "Small tools, maintenance and repair" was also split between "Small tools & equipment" in Cost of Goods Sold and "Maintenance & repairs (non vehicle)" in Overhead Expense.**

## HOW OVERHEAD FIGURES INTO PRICING JOBS

Hope's version of the P&L showed that of the $800,000 in job income, Mike had spent approximately $686,000 on the jobs. This produced a gross profit of $114,000, which is the same as a gross margin of 14.2%. (Refer Figure 3-2.)

| Total Sales | | Job Costs | | Gross Profit |
|---|---|---|---|---|
| $800,000 | - | $686,257 | = | $113,743 |
| | | | | |
| Gross Profit | | Total Sales | | Gross Margin |
| $113,743 | ÷ | $800,000 | = | 14.2% |

**Figure 3-2. To calculate gross margin, divide the gross profit by total sales for the same period.**

Hope said, "From your revised P&L report, we can now see your overhead separated out. Remember, these are the costs that you can count on having each year, and your jobs must bring in enough money to cover them. Last year you spent about $194,500 for overhead expenses. We can convert this into a percentage of sales. It's often easier to look at percentages rather than getting lost in dollars. So another way of looking at your overhead is to say that out of every sales dollar that comes in, you spent almost 24.4 cents on overhead." (Refer Figure 3-3.)

| Overhead | ÷ | Total Sales | = | Overhead as % of sales |
|---|---|---|---|---|
| $194,531 | | $800,000 | | 24.4% |

**Figure 3-3. When overhead costs are separated from job costs, they can be expressed as a percentage of sales.**

"OK," Mike said. "I see that. Is that too high or is that about right?"

"It's less a question of being too high or too low, and more about whether or not your current pricing strategy is adequate to cover it. But now that we've rearranged your P&L, that's pretty easy to check. All we really have to do is to see whether what you have left after paying for your job-related costs is enough to cover your overhead and leave the profit you want."

## RELATING GROSS PROFIT TO YOUR OVERHEAD REQUIREMENTS

Hope circled the gross margin on the P&L. "Here's what you have left from your sales dollars after you've paid your job costs." (Refer Figure 3-4.)

| | |
|---|---|
| Total Sales | $800,000 |
| Total Cost of Goods Sold | -$686,257 |
| Gross Profit | $113,743 |
| Gross Profit Margin | 14.2% |

**Figure 3-4. Gross margin shows, as a percentage, how much remains after job costs have been deducted from total sales dollars.**

Then she circled the figure representing the percentage required to cover overhead costs. (Refer Figure 3-5.)

| | |
|---|---|
| Construction Revenue | $800,000 |
| Total Overhead Expenses | $194,531 |
| Overhead as % of Income | 24.4% |

**Figure 3-5. Expressing overhead costs as a percentage of total sales allows comparison with gross margin.**

"Wow," Mike jumped in. "This looks awful! I see that the 14.2% margin means that I only have 14.2% 'left over' from sales after I pay for job costs. But, I need to have 24.4% left over to cover overhead. I guess that gross margin number should be higher than that overhead percentage. No wonder my company is losing money!"

"So what you're saying is that I need to cut back on my overhead somehow." Mike immediately began reviewing his overhead costs. Maybe he could make some cuts somewhere.

23

## OPTIONS FOR IMPROVING PROFIT

"Not quite, Mike," Hope said. "All this tells you is that your overhead is too high *for the gross margin you're currently producing*. You have some choices for how to solve this. First of all, you *could* try to cut down on your overhead. But that's not a good long-term solution unless you've got some inappropriate expenses, and there's nothing in your P&L that jumps out at me. Relying on keeping your overhead down in order to be profitable simply means you'll threaten your ability to grow your company. Second, you could try to cut down on your production costs by being aggressive about getting more competitive prices from your suppliers and tightening up on your labor efficiency. But there will be limits to that, and it's important to remember that you get what you pay for. Paying the lowest amount for a 2x4 with the result of receiving faulty material and poor delivery service, or getting a cheap but unreliable plumber will certainly cost less in the short run, but ultimately cost more in the long run. Third, you can increase your sales volume. Remember that all of the percentages that we've been looking at are based on dollars of sales. That means that if you increase your sales figures, you'll change the percentages in your favor."

"You mean I need to sell more?" said Mike. "But I'm already scrambling to keep up with the work we have coming in. I don't see how we can add more jobs with the resources we have."

## INCREASE YOUR VOLUME

"When I said that one option is to increase your volume," observed Hope, "your first impulse was to go out and sell more stuff using your existing strategy. But Mike, even if you sell more jobs, if you keep the same pricing system, your gross margin will stay the same and you will probably continue to lose money. What you *really* need to do is to look at changing the way you price things. And that's what we're going to discuss."

Then Hope asked Mike a pivotal question. "Let's say you estimated a job to cost $68,600, what would you price it at?" Mike thought about how he should answer the question. He didn't want to look like an idiot, but Hope seemed eager to help. So he took the plunge. "Well, I would mark it up

15% and then another 10%." He reached for the calculator and come up with about $86,800. (Refer Figure 3-6.)

| | |
|---|---|
| Job costs | $68,600 |
| Add 15% of the costs     + | $10,290 |
| Subtotal | $78,890 |
| | |
| Add 10% of the subtotal  + | $7,889 |
| Total | $86,779 |
| | |
| Sell the job at | $86,779 |

**Figure 3-6. Mike's method of pricing a job successively adds 15% and then 10% to estimated costs.**

Then Hope continued, "If you had priced **ten** jobs that way, you should have brought in $868,000 based on the $686,000 you spent. Since you brought in only $800,000 last year, your income is $68,000 short." (Refer Figure 3-7.)

| | Per job | # of jobs | Estimated totals for year | Actual totals for year | Difference |
|---|---|---|---|---|---|
| Sales | $86,800 | 10 | $868,000 | $800,000 | -$68,000 |
| Costs | $68,600 | 10 | $686,000 | $686,000 | $0 |
| Gross Profit | $18,200 | 10 | $182,000 | $114,000 | -$68,000 |
| Gross Margin | 21.0% | | 21.0% | 14.2% | |

**Figure 3-7. When actual sales and job costs don't reflect the pricing strategy, it's often due to slippage.**

"Wow... I thought I was doing better pricing my jobs to cover costs," Mike said slowly.

## REPORTS CAN SHOW YOU WHAT YOUR SLIPPAGE IS

"Your pricing strategy probably needs to be revised," acknowledged Hope, "but the fact that you thought you were pricing your jobs to produce a higher gross margin is more indicative of a different problem – 'slippage'. In other words, if what it actually costs you is more than what you'd planned on, there's slippage. Sometimes slippage is unavoidable, such as the unexpected increase on product cost on a fixed-price job. Occasionally, it is simply a matter of missed costs or unrealistic labor productivity expectations during the estimating process. But most often, slippage is due to excess hours on the job. Since there are so many sources of slippage and slippage is such a significant problem in this industry, this is the biggest reason to generate and analyze job cost reports. If you don't know what's going wrong, you can't make changes that will help you achieve your financial objectives."

Mike said, "There's one thing I don't get. I understand that there's probably some slippage, as you say. But if my slippage was really low and I stick to my 15+10% markup, wouldn't I make a profit then? I mean, I'm marking up my jobs over 25%, and my overhead is only 24.4%, so there should still be a small profit left over, right?"

## USE NUMBERS TO RUN YOUR BUSINESS

Hope explained that Mike was confusing the markup with the margin. "That's another topic, but we have to wait to discuss this on my next visit. The good news is that once you get a better handle on these numbers, you can use them to price your jobs and manage your change orders so that you can make your jobs profitable."

At this point, Mike was both discouraged and excited. Never in the seventeen months, three weeks, and four days since he'd quit smoking had he so desperately needed to go out back, lean up against the office building in the fresh air, and light up a cigarette. He really needed to just take a few moments to digest what he'd heard, and think about how to better move forward. But he also realized that this was the first time someone had helped him not only look at his numbers but also understand them.

Hope insisted, "This is not as bad as you think. Today we discovered two things. First, your achieved gross margin is insufficient to cover your overhead or produce any profit. Second, your pricing strategy *should* have produced a higher gross margin. The fact that it failed to do so suggests you have slippage. The good news is that with a little more education, some corrections to your accounting, and a commitment to change, I'm convinced that you will be able to turn your company around."

Mike started to think that Hope really understood his business and was going to live up to her name. He was ready now to make the commitment and change for the better. He always knew his numbers could tell him something, he just didn't understand what they were saying.

## *What Mike learned:*

1.  *Reports can be helpful – or not – depending on how the information is organized and presented.*

2.  *Once clear financial data is available in the right format, it doesn't take an analytical genius to see problems.*

3.  *If you can see where a problem is happening, you can probably fix it.*

4.  *Owning and running a construction company effectively has less to do with nail-banging experience than he'd thought.*

## *Self-assessment questions:*

1.  *Are you pricing your jobs intentionally to cover costs + your company's overhead, + your company's target profit?*

2.  *Would you rather go to bed at night <u>wondering</u> or <u>knowing</u> how things are going?*

# CHAPTER 4 – MARKUP AND MARGIN MIX-UP

Hope's next visit was scheduled for the following Tuesday. All that weekend, Mike thought about that $80K that he'd lost the previous year, and wondered whether he was setting himself up to lose even more money on the big Wiley job. On Monday, Mike was distracted. Instead of the usual recurring worries about the jobs in progress, he found himself thinking more about his business as a whole. For his entire professional life, Mike had seen his role as the overseer – the one who made sure things got done from day to day. There had never been time to think about the business itself; there had hardly been time for evenings or the occasional weekend off! But now, for the first time, Mike had a hunch that he *needed* to think about his business instead of his jobs. He was actually looking forward to Hope's next appointment.

"Last time we met, you discovered that your produced margin was 14.3% of sales while your overhead was 24.2% of sales," Hope started the meeting. "It's apparent that this is creating a problem. If you're not able to cover your overhead, then you're certainly not going to make any profit. And, this kind of situation can't last long."

Despite the discouraging nature of this summary, Mike was hopeful that Hope would have a solution. "Yup, that about sums it up. But I still don't understand why I'm losing so much money? If my markup is 25%, and my overhead is 24.2%, shouldn't I be just about breaking even? I think you said it had something to do with confusing markup and margin," he reminded her.

## MARKUP VS. MARGIN

"You're right, Mike! And you're in good company," chuckled Hope. "The two terms are often used – or misused – interchangeably. They're confusing because they describe the relationship among sales, costs, and profit.

"First it's important to note that margins and markups are percentages. The reason to use percentages instead of dollars is that as your total sales change, you can more easily compare percentages instead of dollars. For example, if you have a gross profit of $75,000 one year and $125,000 the next, does that mean you did much better the second year? Maybe, but what if your sales the first year were $200,000 and the second year were $500,000? The first year represents a gross margin of 38% while the next year represents a gross margin of 25%. Were the headaches involved with running a $500,000 company with a 25% gross margin worth that extra $50,000? Or, with the right plan, could you have grown more slowly and managed to keep your gross margin above 35%?" (Refer Figure 4-1.)

| | Year 1 | Margin | Year 2 | Margin |
|---|---|---|---|---|
| Sales | 200,000 | | 500,000 | |
| COGS | 125,000 | | 375,000 | |
| Gross Profit | 75,000 | 38% | 125,000 | 25% |

**Figure 4-1. Bigger sales usually mean bigger headaches, but not necessarily bigger profits. In this example, sales increased by 150% but the gross margin actually dropped 13%.**

"But I'm getting ahead of myself," admitted Hope. "We need to look at the definitions of markup and margin. Let's start with a simple example," said Hope, writing down some numbers.

"I'm going to estimate my job to cost $200 and I'm going to sell the job for $300. Said another way, I'm going to *mark up* my $200 of costs by $100 in order to reach a sale price of $300. (Refer Figure 4-2.) Since the markup is $100 and my job costs are $200, I have a 50% markup because $100 is one-half of $200. So, keep in mind that markup is always based on job *costs*." (Refer Figure 4-3.)

| Job costs | + Markup (50% of Job *costs* ) | = Sale Price |
|-----------|-------------------------------|--------------|
| $200      | $100                          | $300         |

**Figure 4-2 Relationship between costs and sale price.**

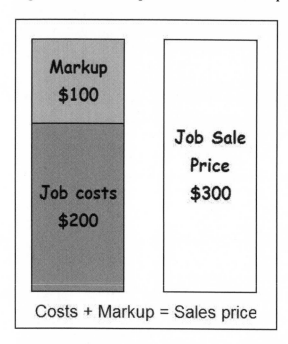

Figure 4-3. Markup is always based on cost.

## MARGIN IS A PERCENTAGE OF SALES

"Now let's look at that $100 of markup from the perspective of the $300 sales price, which in this simple example represents your sales volume."

She continued, "Remember I said that markup is always based on job costs? Well, margin is always based on sales. In this example, your markup of $100 is one-third of your sales price. That means that adding a 50% *markup* to your costs gives you only a 33.3% *gross margin.* In fact, the margin figure will *always* be lower than your markup figure." (Refer Figure 4-4.)

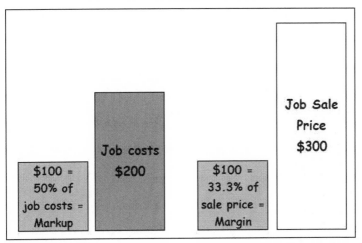

**Figure 4-4. When the $100 is compared with costs, it's called markup. When the $100 is compared with sales price, it's called margin. Margins will always be smaller than markups.**

"Just to make sure, here's the formula," said Hope as she wrote the formula on Mike's whiteboard." (Refer Figure 4-5.)

Markup in $ ÷ Sales Price = Margin
$100            $300        33.3%

**Figure 4-5. Margin is calculated by dividing the markup in dollars by the sales price of the job.**

Hope opened up her binder, pulled out a piece of paper and said, "Mike, I'm going to leave you with a chart that shows the relationship between markup and margin. Remember, margin is always calculated as a percentage of sales, and markup is calculated as a percentage of costs." (Refer to the appendix.)

Mike looked at the figures. "Boy, that can really be confusing, but I think I'm getting it."

## MAKE NUMBERS COMPARABLE

"OK," Hope continued. "Now let's take a look at *your* company's markup and margin numbers. You told me you priced jobs by adding 15% for overhead and 10% for profit; you're adding those percentages to your costs. So is that a markup or a margin?" asked Hope.

"That must be a markup number," answered Mike quickly.

"Absolutely," smiled Hope. "You're using markup numbers. But when we looked at your overhead, we took the total overhead and divided by the sales, and that produced a margin number. So, when you said you marked up your jobs 25% (a markup number) and your overhead was 24% (a margin number) the two are not comparable.

"Now, let's convert your markup to a margin number so we can compare the numbers. If you had a job that cost $100, and you added 15% for overhead and 10% for profit, you would price the job for $126.50. (Refer to Figure 4-6.) This is working up from costs, using markup percentages to get to sales price."

| | |
|---|---|
| Job Costs | $100.00 |
| Add 15% for overhead | $15.00 |
| Subtotal | $115.00 |
| Add 10% for profit | $11.50 |
| Total Sales Price | $126.50 |

**Figure 4-6. Mike's method of calculating the sales price of a job based on adding 15% + 10% to the estimated costs.**

"OK, that's the first point. Then, assuming you had no slippage, and hit your budget, let's see what margin this job would produce." Hope created a spreadsheet to show Mike how to calculate these numbers and percentages. (Refer Figure 4-7.)

| | | |
|---|---|---|
| Sale Price | $126.50 | |
| Job Costs | $100.00 | |
| Gross Profit | $26.50 | |
| | | |
| Gross Margin | 20.95% | (26.5 ÷ 126.50) |
| Markup | 26.50% | (26.5 ÷ 100.00) |

**Figure 4-7. To calculate markup, divide gross profit in dollars by job costs. To calculate margin, divide gross profit in dollars by income (sales price).**

Mike looked up and said, "Holy cow! Does that really mean that if I markup my jobs with the 15 and 10% I've been using, I can't even get a 21% margin? And when I compare that 21% margin to the 24% overhead, now I can see why I lost $80K last year!"

"Right you are!" said Hope. "And there are several ways to address this problem. First of all, we know that current markup strategy *should* be producing about a 21% gross margin. Since the revised P&L shows only a 14% achieved gross margin, the discrepancy must be due to slippage. Let's look at your numbers a little closer and see where you might consider making changes. We need to decide if you should lower your overhead, increase your prices, or minimize slippage. Let's address each one separately. Because slippage is tied to effective production methods, and right now we're looking at your numbers, we'll address this issue later."

## USE HISTORICAL INFORMATION TO CREATE TARGETS

"We'll start by taking another look at my revised copy of your P&L from last year. To keep things simple, I'm going to create a summary version (refer Figure 4-8) in addition to the detailed version. Last year, you spent about $194,500 on overhead costs. Do you think that your overhead will change significantly this year compared with last?"

| | | |
|---|---|---|
| Total Income | $800,000 | |
| Total Cost of Goods Sold | $686,257 | |
| | | |
| Gross Profit | $113,743 | |
| Gross Margin | 14.20% | ($113,743 ÷ $800,000) |
| | | |
| Total Overhead Expenses | $194,531 | |
| Overhead as % of Income | 24.20% | $194,531 ÷ $800,000) |
| | | |
| Net Profit from Operations | -$80,789 | |
| Net Profit Margin | -10.10% | (-$80,789 ÷ $800,000) |

**Figure 4-8. Simplified version of Mike's P&L from last year showing summary totals and calculated percentages.**

Mike looked at the expanded version of the revised Profit and Loss that

Hope had created on her last visit. He scanned the various costs: advertising, office supplies, rent, utilities, Marci's and his salaries…he'd certainly not had any unusual expenses last year, and he guessed that this year would be a repeat of last. "No," he replied. "It'll probably be around the same."

"OK," said Hope. "Let's do a quick calculation based on some assumptions. First, we'll assume that your overhead costs remain the same. Second, we'll assume that you spend the same amount for job costs. Finally, here's the $64,000 question. What would you like to earn in net profit? Notice that I'm treating net profit just like it was a cost to you. Remember, this is the reward you get for the risks involved in being in business."

Mike wrestled with the question. First of all, it felt more like some quiz show called "Name Your Profit!" than something achievable. Second, given the opportunity to say a number out loud, Mike felt uncomfortable. What was fair? What was reasonable? He didn't want Hope to think he was greedy. On the other hand, he'd put years of hard work and sacrifice into this business and surely deserved some payback. Hesitantly, Mike asked, "Well, $64,000 sounds like a really good number; is that too much?"

## TARGET NET PROFIT PLUS TARGET OVERHEAD EQUALS TARGET GROSS PROFIT

Instead of answering, Hope merely remarked, "OK, let's take that as a working figure and see where that takes us." Mike liked her non-judgmental approach. Also, his curiosity was piqued!

"Mike, this is the only information we need in order to estimate what your sales would *need to be* in order to cover these costs because your total sales figure will always contain *only* these components." (Refer Figure 4-9.)

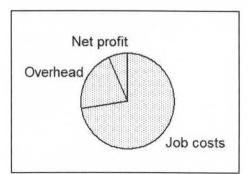

**Figure 4-9. Total sales will always be the sum of job costs + overhead + profit.**

## DETERMINE TARGET SALES VOLUME

"When we plug in the numbers, we can see what your sales figure for this year should be in order to cover these costs." (Refer Figure 4-10.)

| | |
|---|---|
| Job costs | $686,257 |
| Overhead | $194,531 |
| Net profit | $64,000 |
| Sales | $944,788 |

**Figure 4-10. Adding anticipated job costs + anticipated overhead + desired profit produces a target sales figure.**

"What?" exclaimed Mike. "You mean I have to sell almost $945,000 this year? It'll never happen. I thought I might make a little more than last year because of the Wiley job, but not *that much* more. What am I going to do?"

## COST, OVERHEAD OR PROFIT – PICK ONE!

"You're probably right, Mike," acknowledged Hope. "It may not be realistic to plan on that big an increase. So we need to be brutally honest when looking at your options. After all, we only have three elements to manipulate: job costs, overhead, and profit. One option would be to try to lower your overhead. A second option would be to produce your jobs more efficiently, which would lower your job costs. A third option would be to accept a lower profit." Hope paused to let the information sink in. Then she continued with a twinkle, "By the way, Mike, although you didn't do it intentionally, the third option is exactly the one you chose last year.

"Each of these options would reduce the required sales volume. Let's see how a 10% reduction in each one would play out as we work up from the costs to determine sales." (Refer Figure 4-11.)

| | | Option 1 costs by 10% | Option 2 overhead by 10% | Option 3 Reduce profit by 10% |
|---|---|---|---|---|
| Job costs | $686,257 | $617,631 | $686,257 | $686,257 |
| Overhead | $194,531 | $194,531 | $175,078 | $194,531 |
| Net profit | $64,000 | $64,000 | $64,000 | $57,600 |
| Sales | $944,788 | $876,162 | $925,335 | $938,388 |

**Figure 4-11. Effect on target sales volume of reducing job costs, overhead, and net profit by 10%.**

"As you can see, reducing your job costs by 10% gives you the biggest cut to your sales volume because job costs are the biggest slice in your sales pie. As we continue to look at your company, we should find ways to improve your efficiency. But this is just one component of the total solution.

"Another solution involves increasing your markup. Doing this would increase your sales volume without forcing you to make cuts. Let's see what your markup would need to be in order to keep your estimated costs intact. I'm going to take that target sales figure of $944,788 and rearrange the information in the same format as your P&L. Then we can use the information to calculate what your markup would need to be." (Refer Figure 4-12.)

| | | |
|---|---|---|
| Sales | $944,788 | |
| COGS | $686,257 | |
| Gross Profit | $258,531 | |
| Overhead | $194,531 | |
| Target Net Profit | $64,000 | |
| | | |
| Dollars of markup | $258,531 | (same as the gross profit) |
| Markup % | 37.67% | ($258,531 ÷ $686,257) |

**Figure 4-12. Calculate markup by dividing estimated gross profit by job costs.**

Mike looked intently at the results. "You mean that if my job costs and overhead stay the same, and I increase my markup to about 38%, I'd actually wind up making my $64,000 target net profit and my sales volume would grow by *that much*?"

"Close, Mike. If this were January 1st, and you hadn't yet sold any work at your old markup, then that statement would be accurate given the usual 'ifs': no slippage, no overhead cost overruns, and so forth. However, it's already the end of the first quarter, and you've sold what may be your biggest job of the year at your old markup. Therefore, you can't expect to get these results *this year*. However, you can make a start. If you raise your markup on new jobs, increase production efficiency, and look for additional cost-cutting opportunities, you should be able to at least break even this year, and perhaps even make a little profit."

Mike sighed and said, "So, it's not all gloom and doom?"

"Certainly not," Hope smiled encouragingly. "In fact, let's look at the numbers one more way. If we keep your overhead of around $195,000 and add the $64,000 net profit, we come up with a total of about $259,000. That number is the same as the gross profit that you need to make in order to meet your overhead obligation and net profit goal. We can use this number to determine your sales goal." (Refer Figure 4-13.)

| Overhead | $195,000 | Sales | $ XXXX |
|----------|----------|-------|--------|
| Net Profit | $64,000 | Job Costs | - YYY |
| | $259,000 | = Gross Profit | $259,000 |

**Figure 4-13. The sum of projected overhead and net profit should be equal to the projected gross profit in dollars.**

"First, let's look at your estimated gross margin of about 21%. Do you remember where I got that number?"

"I sure do," said Mike. "You showed me that if I price a job with a 15% plus 10% markup, I will end up with a 21% margin."

"Yup," confirmed Hope. "So, in order to achieve the gross profit goal of $259,000 with a gross margin of 21%, you divide the gross profit by the gross margin to produce the sales volume. This means that if you really wanted to earn a net profit of $64,000 *and* your overhead didn't change, *and* you were able to come in on budget on your jobs, you'd have to sell about $1.2 million dollars in work per year." (Refer Figure 4-14.)

| Gross Profit | ÷ Margin | = Sales Volume |
|--------------|----------|----------------|
| $259,000 | 21% | $1,233,333 |

**Figure 4-14. To determine a target sales volume ($), divide gross profit by the estimated gross margin (%).**

"No way!" sputtered Mike. "I can't possibly sell that much. This is getting worse by the minute!"

"Hold on, Mike. Don't panic yet," said Hope reassuringly. "That sales figure is based on your current estimated gross margin of 21%. Let's see how the numbers might change if you increase your gross margin to 32%, which is more typical of successful remodeling companies."

## DIFFERENT MARGINS MEAN DIFFERENT TARGET SALES

"So, if we take the $259,000 and divide by 32%, notice that you only have to sell around $810,000 – pretty much your current volume." (Refer Figure 4-15.)

| Gross Profit | ÷ Margin | = Sales Volume |
|:---:|:---:|:---:|
| $259,000 | 32% | $809,375 |

**Figure 4-15. Target sales volume will decrease as estimated gross margin increases.**

"And with a 33% achieved margin, you'd actually need to sell *less* than you did last year. (Refer Figure 4-16.) And this brings us back to the first simple example we worked with – when I showed you that a 50% markup produced a 33% margin."

| Gross Profit | Gross Margin | Sales Volume |
|:---:|:---:|:---:|
| $259,000 | 21% | $1,233,333 |
| $259,000 | 25% | $1,036,000 |
| $259,000 | 30% | $863,333 |
| $259,000 | 33% | $784,848 |

**Figure 4-16. Increasing the margin decreases the sales volume required to cover overhead and net profit.**

"Are you telling me," Mike gasped, "that I need to use a 50% markup? I'll never sell another job!"

"The numbers don't lie, Mike," said Hope. "I *am* telling you that if you want to cover your company's overhead costs *and* make a profit, you will need to do one of two things: either reach a specific sales target or achieve a specific gross margin target. I caution you not to try to increase your sales volume as a way of fixing your financial troubles. You know the old joke: 'What I lose in profit, I can make up in volume'. A better solution is to use the correct markup right from the start to help you reach your targets. The markup that you need to use in your company will be different from the markup that your competitor across town may be using. The point is that markup isn't about making the selling price look good to your customer, or trying to match your competitor's hourly labor rate. You need to price your jobs according to a plan that includes *your* overhead and *your* profit. It's got to be a plan for *your* company."

Once again, Hope had produced mixed feelings in Mike. He was excited about the prospect of being able to actually *plan* on making profit, but horrified at the thought of *increasing* his markup, and staying competitive. Was he learning about this stuff too late? Mike's heart was pounding now, but Hope did not seem to be discouraged by the figures she was seeing. Mike decided that if Hope wasn't in a panic about his business, maybe he shouldn't be either.

As the enormity of what he'd just learned sank in, Mike had only one question to ask: "So are you also going to tell me how I'm ever going to *sell any jobs* at a 50% markup? I can't make this company profitable if I go out of business because I can't sell the work."

"That's a totally different topic," smiled Hope encouragingly. "I suggest you look into sales training, or locate a consultant who specializes in sales and marketing for the construction industry. But the good news is that many remodelers are already successfully selling work with markups at least this high. And sometimes, it's better to do less work with a higher margin."

Mike let out a big sigh, "This is a lot of information. But it actually is starting to make sense! Why my accountant never explained it this way I'll never understand. But I'm going to think about all these numbers: margin, markup, gross profit, net profit and sales volume."

"I agree," said Hope. "Let's call it a day for now."

### What Mike learned:

1. *Markup % and margin % aren't the same thing (although markup dollars and gross profit dollars are the same thing).*

2. *He was more content before he knew how much trouble he was in, but he would have continued to be content right up until it was too late!*

3. What companies sell their work for depends on that specific company's costs.

4. Numbers don't lie. They can be used to create targets and build a plan around them.

5. The numbers he got from his accountant weren't the ones he needed in order to create a strategy.

### *Self-assessment questions:*

1. Do you know your overhead numbers?

2. Do you have a target net profit figure?

3. Do you know what your gross margin was for the past 12 months? Do you know what your gross margin needs to be for the next 12 months?

4. Is your company making the profit you expect and deserve?

5. Should you consider sales and marketing training?

6. Will you read on or bury your head back in the sand?

# CHAPTER 5 – SHOW ME THE MONEY!

When Hope returned on Friday, Mike was in a panic. He'd spent the last three days trying to figure out how he could sell anything with such a high markup. He practically pounced on Hope when she walked in the door and demanded an answer. Hope calmly explained, "Mike, I'm glad you've been thinking about all that we've been discussing. Let's look at your jobs to see where there are opportunities for additional markup. With all that we've been analyzing, and with your concerns about the Wiley job, why don't we start by looking at that budget?"

Mike showed Hope a spreadsheet for the Wiley Job. He started to ask a question, but Hope held up her hand and said, "Hmmm, just give me a minute to see how you've arrived at these numbers."

## ESTIMATING LABOR DOLLARS

Hope immediately zeroed in on the labor dollars. She asked Mike how he figured the cost of labor. Mike replied, "I estimate the number of hours I think it will take and multiply that by my billing rate. Since I pay $25 per hour for each person on my field crew, and charge $80 per hour, I figure there should be some profit in that." Then he paused and smiled. "I always use a high labor rate because I never know how many hours it will really take, and I use that to build in a cushion."

Hope smiled again. "Mike, your markup of 15% and 10% is put on top of a markup for labor. This is good news and bad news. The good news is that you are actually using a higher markup than you said, so that 47% markup isn't so far away. The bad news is that this additional markup is only available if you meet your labor budget. Let me show you some numbers."

## HIDDEN PROFIT INSIDE BILLING RATES

She then created a quick spreadsheet for Mike. (Refer Figure 5-1.) "Let's create a simple budget for a small job. Let's say that it will have $30,000 for material and $30,000 for subcontractors. Also, let's say it takes two guys four weeks to do the job. At your $80 billing rate the budget for labor is $25,600. Then add on your 15% and 10% to come up with your sales price."

| Labor (320 x $80) | $25,600 |
|---|---|
| Materials | $30,000 |
| Subcontractors | $30,000 |
| Subtotal | $85,600 |
| Add Overhead (15%) | $12,840 |
| Subtotal | $98,440 |
| Add Profit (10%) | $9,844 |
| Total Price | **$108,284** |

**Figure 5-1. Sample job budget: labor portion calculated at charge-out rate.**

Hope continued, "Looking at these numbers, do you think you might try and sell this job for $110,000?" Mike agreed. Hope went on, "Now, let's figure out the gross margin on this job. The gross profit from this would be $110,000 less $85,600 which is $24,400. That number divided by the sales price of $110,000 equals 22%. (Refer Figure 5-2.) Just about what we've been looking at."

| Sales Price | - Job Costs | = Gross Profit | ÷ Sales Price | = Gross Margin |
|---|---|---|---|---|
| $110,000 | $85,600 | $24,400 | $110,000 | 22% |

**Figure 5-2. Sample job margin calculation.**

## CALCULATING MARGIN BASED ON GROSS WAGE

"However, I don't think it really costs $80 per hour for you to put an employee out on the job. Let's revise the budget numbers based what you pay per hour. This time we'll take your $25/hr cost figure and multiply by the total hours." And Hope reworked the numbers on a strictly cost basis. (Refer Figure 5-3.)

| | |
|---|---|
| Labor (320 x $25) | $8,000 |
| Materials | $30,000 |
| Subcontractors | $30,000 |
| Subtotal | $68,000 |

**Figure 5-3. Sample job budget: labor portion calculated at unburdened rate.**

"Assuming we sell the job for the same price of $110,000, can you tell me the margin on this job?"

Mike was eager to answer the question. He punched some numbers into the calculator. "First, if I subtract $68,000 from $110,000, the gross profit should be $42,000. Then let me divide $42,000 by $110,000." Then, he looked up and said with a grin, "38%?"

| Sales Price | - Job Costs | = Gross Profit | ÷ Sales Price | = Gross Margin |
|---|---|---|---|---|
| $110,000 | $68,000 | $42,000 | $110,000 | 38% |

**Figure 5-4. Calculating gross margin using unburdened wage.**

Hope returned the smile and said, "Yes, absolutely right!"

Mike said, "So that means that I'm marking up my jobs 38%?" Then, before Hope could answer he said, "What a minute. I just confused markup and margin again. That means that I should be earning a gross margin of 38%! That's even bigger than the 32% target margin that we came up with before."

## INCLUDING THE LABOR BURDEN IN THE ESTIMATE

Hope was pleased to see that Mike had corrected himself. "Wait a minute Mike, there's a little more to the story. Just because you pay an employee $25 per hour, it doesn't mean that it costs you only $25 per hour. There are employer-paid costs that you need to consider, such as payroll taxes, workers' compensation, and liability insurance just to name a few. These are called labor burdens, and if you add those costs to your budgeted labor, you will get a better idea of the true costs to run the job. We'll have to look at your specific burdens another day, but for rough estimating purposes, let's just assume a very modest burden rate of 35% to account for payroll taxes and other costs that vary among companies. That means we're going to add 35% to your gross wage figure. So for every dollar you pay an employee, we're going to assume that it actually costs you $1.35.

"Let's look at the numbers on this job one more time, using a burdened labor rate." This time Hope added burden to the labor cost. (Refer Figure 5-5.)

| | |
|---|---|
| Labor (320 x $25 x 1.35) | $10,800 |
| Materials | $30,000 |
| Subcontractors | $30,000 |
| Subtotal | $70,800 |

**Figure 5-5. Sample job budget: labor portion calculated at estimated 35% burden rate.**

Without Hope even asking, Mike jumped on his calculator to come up with the margin. (Refer Figure 5-6.) "That means the job should produce a margin of 36%. Am I right?"

| Sales Price | - Job Costs | = Gross Profit | ÷ Sales Price | = Gross Margin |
|---|---|---|---|---|
| $110,000 | $70,800 | $39,200 | $110,000 | 36% |

**Figure 5-6. Calculating gross margin using 35% burdened labor cost.**

Hope agreed that Mike was really starting to understand this. Hope didn't want to quash Mike's enthusiasm, but she had to provide a reality check. "Yes, Mike, that means that your jobs should be producing a 36% margin. But that is not the case. We saw that you're coming in at around 14%. There are three reasons the numbers don't agree. First, when I revised your own financial statements, I used that 35% burden. And I still came up with a margin of 14%. This tells me that you're probably spending more hours on the jobs than you've budgeted, another source of slippage."

Mike nodded his head. "Yeah, I already knew that. But I thought that since I used the $80 billing rate in the budget, I had a lot of extra dollars so that when we went over on hours, it didn't really matter. I can see now that it does."

## JOBS HAVE LABOR, MATERIALS AND SUBCONTRACTOR COSTS – WHAT'S THE MARKUP?

Hope went on. "The second problem is that the numbers I used in the example are pretty equally split between materials, subs and labor. You have a hidden markup in your labor, but what happens when a job has significantly more subcontractor costs? For jobs that have a lower percentage of labor dollars, you'll have a lower hidden markup in that labor and a lower sales price. I had a client who was very profitable doing small kitchen and bath remodels and who inflated labor like you do. Then, one of his customers liked his work so much that he hired my client to build a custom home. All of a sudden, there were a lot more dollars wrapped up in subcontractors and materials, and less in labor. He estimated the job the same way as he had always done. And because he was missing the cushion added to labor, he lost his shirt!"

Mike started to sweat again. The Wiley job was bigger than his previous jobs, and that was exactly the case. He'd have to do a better job of keeping on budget on this job!

## CONSIDER MISCELLANEOUS COSTS

Hope went on to explain the third reason why his margin was so low. "Finally, we need to look at your job costs a little more closely. Do all your job costs produce revenue? Do you have miscellaneous production-related costs such as shop cleaning, office repairs or warranty work that will never be invoiced? Do you have extra material or subcontractor costs that don't really belong to a job or don't really make any money? If you do, then because these costs are classified as Cost of Goods Sold, they will lower your margin even further."

She showed him the detail of his account called "Licenses and Permits" and discovered that almost $14,300 was spent on a series of permits he had pulled for his jobs. Hope asked Mike what the markup was on permits and Mike stammered, "I didn't think I could mark them up!"

Hope replied, "Yes, many builders do not mark up permit costs. But I just want you to know that any costs that are billed to the customer with no associated overhead or profit will dilute your margin. So consider who carries the permit risk and who should pay the permit fees. If you're paying the fees, then consider adding a markup. Or perhaps you should have your customers pay those fees directly."

Just as Mike felt like his head was about to explode, Hope said, "That's enough for today. Just to summarize, we need to revise your estimates to show your actual labor costs, not your labor billing rates. I call what you've been doing 'hybrid estimating.' In other words, some parts of your estimate, like materials and subcontractors, were based on costs. But labor was based on your chargeout rate instead of costs. It's difficult to apply an overall markup figure to your estimated costs when not all the numbers you have represent actual costs. Once we've got labor cost figures instead of your chargeout rate in the estimate, we can increase your markup without actually increasing your sales price. Over the next couple of visits, I'm going to help you see how you can revise your Wiley job budget based on your burdened labor rates, not your billing rates. Then, we can set up QuickBooks to track your job costs. Ultimately our goal is to create an estimate with the same assumptions as your job costing. That way, we can compare apples to apples. Right now, I think you've been comparing apples to pineapples…"

Mike finished her sentence with, "Yeah, and that's left a bad taste in my mouth!"

### *What Mike learned:*

1. *If you use labor cost instead of labor billing rates, you must use a higher markup to arrive at the same sales price.*

2. *Perhaps he's not as far away from the calculated markup figure as he thought.*

3. *Using labor billing rates in an estimate leads you to squander labor hours or reduce motivation to correct them.*

4. *Mike really needs to know how much it actually costs to put an employee in the field.*

5. *Mike should seek to improve his ability to estimate the real number of hours required, not try to fudge for it in his labor rate.*

### *Self-assessment questions:*

1. *Do you estimate based on costs, including the true cost of your labor?*

2. *Do you use multiple markups or a consistent markup applied to each type of costs (i.e. burdened labor, materials, subs, etc.)?*

3. *Have you noticed any difference in job profitability depending on how much labor the job did or did not include compared with materials and subs?*

4. *Are you comfortable about "guessing" the cost of being in business?*

5. *Should you keep reading or go find a job working for someone else?*

# CHAPTER 6 – TOP OF THE CHARTS IT IS

Mike was actually looking forward to Hope's next visit. She was really making sense and had allayed some of his fears about the Wiley job. He was optimistic that he could manage the labor better, and keep within the budgeted hours.

"So, what tricks do you have up your sleeve for me today?" Mike quipped.

"Well," Hope responded. "I think now we pretty much agree that you want to stay on track for the Wiley job. And we can have your software help you do that. But first we need to fix your financial statements so they tell you what you need to know.

"Remember when I put together that revised spreadsheet of your Profit and Loss Statement? You should be able to get that information directly from your accounting system. I want to show you how I came up with the 14% margin and see if you agree with my numbers. We need to be on the same page as to what is considered a job cost and what is overhead."

## COST OF GOODS SOLD

"Job costs belong in a section of the Profit and Loss Statement called Cost of Goods Sold, which is often referred to as COGS," Hope explained. "This is a term that may not make much sense to a contractor, but historically it comes from the manufacturing industry and standard financial reports continue to categorize production costs as Cost of Goods Sold. You can think of COGS as being the same as job costs." She continued jokingly, "In fact, some contractors think it also means 'Cost of Goods Stole'! To further confuse the issue, many people refer to these as 'direct costs' since they are directly connected with job production. In your accounting software, all your production costs or job costs should be set up as Cost of Goods Sold type accounts."

"Let's start with a sample P&L and talk about some commonly used terms. Costs are often designated as 'above the line' or 'below the line.'" Hope showed Mike exactly what that line was; it was the line that subtotaled all COGS. (Refer Figure 6-1.) "Any costs above the line would be subtracted from the selling price to obtain the gross profit. Any costs below that line would be included in the Overhead Expenses section. The amount left after the overhead is paid is called net profit, or the 'bottom line.'" Mike knew he'd heard costs referred to in that way, but had never really seen why that distinction was so important. Now, he really understood this issue.

| Income | |
|---|---|
| **Total Income** | **$ 1,300,000** |
| | |
| **Cost of Goods Sold** | |
| Labor Costs | $300,000 |
| Materials Costs | $240,000 |
| Subcontractor Costs | $250,000 |
| Equipment Rental Costs | $37,500 |
| Other Direct Costs | $12,500 |
| **Total COGS** | **$840,000** |
| | |
| **Gross Profit ($)** | $460,000 |
| | |
| **Overhead Expenses** | |
| Advertising | $26,000 |
| Office Supplies | $6,500 |
| Postage | $1,500 |
| Rent | $18,000 |
| Utilities | $6,500 |

**Figure 6-1. "The Line" in a fictional P&L.**

Hope showed Mike how she'd separated out his job costs from his overhead costs to create that spreadsheet on their first meeting. He could see how separating these costs could really help. "Why don't we create different COGS accounts for the different type of work that I do, such as framing and finish? Then I could get even more detailed information on jobs."

## INTRODUCTION TO PARALLELISM

"Whoa," said Hope with a smile. "It's great that you want to get more detail on the jobs, but that's not done inside your Profit and Loss Statement. The P&L is a standard financial report and needs to be kept simple. The job costing is done elsewhere. You will be able to get more detail about your job costs if you use your financial software properly. For most construction specific software, you use another system for job costs. Different software uses different names, such as items, cost codes, work phases, or other categorizations but it's always used to provide the job cost breakdown outside the P&L. But let's keep on track with just the Profit and Loss Statement for now. One thing you might consider doing is setting up separate Income accounts that mirror your Cost of Goods Sold accounts. For example, if you could break out your Job Income account into separate accounts for Labor Income, Material Income, Subcontractor Income, and any other relevant income categories, then you could measure your gross margin for each of these subcategories of COGS." (Refer Figure 6-2)

| Income | | |
|---|---|---|
| Labor Income | $ | 400,000 |
| Materials Income | $ | 400,000 |
| Subcontractor Income | $ | 400,000 |
| Equipment Rental Income | $ | 75,000 |
| Other Direct Income | $ | 25,000 |
| **Total Income** | **$** | **1,300,000** |
| | | |
| **Cost of Goods Sold** | | |
| Labor Costs | $ | 300,000 |
| Materials Costs | $ | 240,000 |
| Subcontractor Costs | $ | 250,000 |
| Equipment Rental Costs | $ | 37,500 |
| Other Direct Costs | $ | 12,500 |
| **Total COGS** | **$** | **840,000** |
| | | |
| **Gross Profit ($)** | **$** | **460,000** |
| Gross Margin (%) | | **35.38%** |

**Figure 6-2. Chart of Accounts with parallelism between income and COGS accounts.**

Hope went on to tell Mike about another contractor who didn't know the source of his income. He had made lots of money remodeling, but had then tried to move into the framing business, framing a 250-unit apartment complex. He had no idea that he'd been making his entire margin on the subcontract portion of the remodeling work. Now, as a framer, he no longer used subcontractors and only had his own labor and materials to produce a profit. After he lost almost a million dollars on the project, he called Hope for help. But by then, it was too late.

## VALUE OF PARALLELISM – MARGIN BY COST TYPE

Mike thought this made a lot of sense. He thought he was making money on jobs, but he wasn't sure where the money was coming from. Hope showed Mike how the margins for each income and COGS category could be easily determined by exporting the P&L to Excel and adding a few formulas. (Refer Figure 6-3.) Mike said, "Yes, I can really see how this can help me use my Profit and Loss to see where I'm making money." Then, with a rueful laugh, he added, "Or losing money!"

|  | Sales Price - | Job Costs = | Gross Profit ÷ | Sales Price = | Gross Margin |
|---|---|---|---|---|---|
| Labor | $400,000 | $300,000 | $100,000 | $400,000 | 25.00% |
| Material | $400,000 | $240,000 | $160,000 | $400,000 | 40.00% |
| Sucontractor | $400,000 | $250,000 | $150,000 | $400,000 | 37.50% |
| Equipment | $75,000 | $37,500 | $37,500 | $75,000 | 50.00% |
| Other | $25,000 | $12,500 | $12,500 | $25,000 | 50.00% |
| Total | $1,300,000 | $840,000 | $460,000 | $1,300,000 | 35.38% |

**Figure 6-3. P&L in Excel with additional calculations to show achieved margin by category.**

Hope replied, "Great. But now let's be very clear on what we're trying to do. I've provided a sample Chart of Accounts that I want you to review. Shortly, I'll also be asking you to create a different list: a list of items that you can use to classify job costs *outside* your Profit and Loss Statement. These items should be very general in nature, such as Site Work, Framing, and Electrical. They should mirror the way you do your estimating and we'll be discussing how to do this during my next visit."

# INVOLVING THE WHOLE TEAM

Hope paused to make sure Mike was paying attention. "You know, Mike, we've been spending a lot of time together looking ahead at making changes. But any changes will affect your team, and it's really important to keep others in the loop. I suggest that before our next meeting, you meet with Marci and fill her in on what we've been talking about. She's a key player and you need to be sure she's on board with all of this. Why don't you show her the spreadsheet with the Chart of Accounts revisions and explain to her why we're going to make these changes. Next time I come, I'll spend some time with Marci and show her how to make these changes in QuickBooks. Please be sure you let her know I expect to spend some time with her during my next visit. She should allow 60-90 minutes for meeting with me. I'd also like to ask Frankie to join us during the second part of my visit. As your Project Manager he also needs to understand job costing in QuickBooks, and I'd like to include him when we discuss this next time."

### *What Mike learned:*

1.  *All job-related costs (direct costs) should be in their own section called Cost of Goods Sold.*

2.  *The Profit and Loss Statement can be used to help you find where you are making money (or losing it).*

3.  *Line item job detail should be outside the Chart of Accounts and the P&L in a separate report of itemized costs.*

### *Self-assessment questions:*

1.  *Are your job-related accounts mixed in with your overhead accounts?*

2.  *Are you trying to job cost through your P&L by having lots of detailed job-related accounts?*

3.  *Could you benefit from having a Chart of Accounts set up with parallelism between income and COGS accounts?*

# CHAPTER 7 – SHARING THE ENTHUSIASM

After Hope left, Mike was pretty excited about sharing his newfound knowledge about the Chart of Accounts with Marci. He was confident that she would immediately grasp the significance of arranging the Chart of Accounts to separate job-related costs from overhead costs. After all, as a bookkeeper, she'd probably be really interested in getting more useful reports. Marci was keyboarding up a storm when he approached, and he waited somewhat impatiently for her to stop. "Marci, Hope has explained to me that in order to better understand how I'm making and spending my money, we really need to rearrange the Chart of Accounts."

## INTRODUCING CHANGES

He brought out the spreadsheet Hope had created during her first visit, and pointed out those accounts that would need to be changed. "See, we had all our costs in one section. Hope said we should separate out the job costs from the overhead costs. She suggested we move a bunch of these accounts into a separate category called Cost of Goods Sold. For example, we have subcontractors down here as an expense, but we only need subs for working on jobs, so it really belongs up in job costs, not in overhead. Once we change around this Chart of Accounts, then I'll be able to see my gross margin right on a P&L. That's going to be *so helpful*. Oh, and we're probably also going to need some new income accounts. Hope says that we can actually track what we charge and spend on similar categories and that will help me know whether or not I'm getting a consistent margin. For example, if I have a Cost of Goods Sold account for subs, then I'll also have an Income account for subs, and then I'll know how much gross profit I'm making on subs. It's pretty cool!" Mike beamed.

## MEETING RESISTANCE TO CHANGE

Marci barely glanced at Hope's spreadsheet. With her glasses resting low on her nose, she looked up at Mike with that blank stare he'd seen many times before. "Well, I know you've been spending lots of time with that lady. So, when you figure it out, just let me know. I've got stuff to do."

"OK..." said Mike, slowly. He remembered what Hope had said about Marci being a key player, and her lack of enthusiasm worried him. Her tone had somewhat deflated him. "Oh, and Hope asked me to let you know that she'll need about an hour and a half of your time during her next visit. I think she wants to talk with you in more detail about some changes."

"Uh-huh," said Marci in a distracted tone. The rhythm of her keyboard clicks continued steadily as Mike walked away. Mike wondered to himself why she didn't have the same enthusiasm he did.

***What Mike learned:***

1.  *Enthusiasm isn't always contagious.*

2.  *People don't always respond the way you expect them to.*

***Self-assessment questions:***

1.  *When you think about making changes, how and when do you involve your staff?*

2.  *Do you foster teamwork and actively ask for input from your employees?*

# CHAPTER 8 – ALL ABOARD!

When Hope arrived for the next appointment, Mike was waiting for her at the door. "I did what you suggested and discussed the Chart of Account changes with Marci, and it didn't exactly go the way I expected it to," he began.

"What happened?" asked Hope.

"Well, instead of being interested in what you and I have been talking about, she treated my explanation as more of an interruption," Mike explained. "You said – and I agree – that she's an important member of the team, and I guess I expected her to act like more of a team member."

Hope thought he seemed a little anxious. "Did you expect her to show a lot of interest in these changes when she doesn't see how they might affect her? After all, if Marci came to you and announced that she was going to print all of the timecards on yellow paper instead of white because that would help her be more efficient, would you get very excited about that?"

Mike had to admit that as long as the timecards kept coming in on time, he really didn't care what color they were. "But I told her that the reports would be more valuable after the Chart of Accounts gets changed. Shouldn't that matter to her?"

## WILLINGNESS TO CHANGE MEANS UNDERSTANDING THE CHANGE

"Once the accounts are rearranged, will she have to do anything different to enter data or run the reports?" asked Hope. Without waiting for Mike to answer, she continued, "No. So, like you and the paper color, whatever you decide to do that helps *you* out is OK with her. That is, right up until the changes we make start to impact *her* work. That's when you should be prepared to meet resistance. As I promised last time, I'm going to spend some time with Marci today and try to get a handle on what she thinks about this process. In fact, I'm going to set that up with her right now. Oh, and you *did* let her know that I need time with her today, right?"

"Oh, I told her all right." Waiting to see Marci's reaction, Mike watched Hope walk over to Marci's desk. Maybe Hope could boost Marci's enthusiasm; maybe Marci would see the advantages and get excited about being part of the improvements.

## INVOLVING THE BOOKKEEPER

"Hi, Marci," said Hope. "Would you have a few minutes this morning for me to talk with you? I know that Mike has told you a little bit about some changes we will make to your accounting file, and I thought you might have some questions about them."

Marci eyes never left her computer monitor. "I'm pretty busy today. I need to enter all the timecards because payroll is run tomorrow, and Mike likes me to keep on top of entering bills. Maybe another day."

"I appreciate that your time is valuable, Marci, and I don't want to put you behind. On the other hand, I believe Mike told you I'd be asking for some time with you today. I was hoping you'd be able to arrange your work today to let that happen as planned."

The keyboarding stopped. Marci sighed and then met Hope's eyes. "Well, to tell you the truth, I don't have any questions about what Mike told me. Whatever he decides, that's what will happen. After all, he's the boss. I frankly don't see how this involves me."

Hope nodded and then smiled. "Yes, I can see how the changes to the Chart of Accounts won't appear to affect you much, but I'm sure that Mike will ask *you* to make the changes, and I thought I'd give you a heads-up on some of the challenges you might encounter when it comes time for you to make those revisions. Also, changing the Chart of Accounts is a *structural change* and you're right, it won't affect you. When you enter a bill for small tools, for example, it won't make any difference to you whether that account is an Expense-type account or a Cost of Goods Sold-type account. However, after the structural changes are in place, we're also going to be revising some procedures, and that *will* affect you directly. I thought it would be good for us to spend some time together so I can provide a preview of what's coming down the pike."

## KEEP THE TEAM INFORMED

Marci's face fell at the mention of any change that involved her. She looked over at Mike to make sure he was in his office and out of earshot. When she spoke, there was a hint of anxiety in her voice. "Wait a minute. Mike has gotten all excited about things in the past, and I wind up being told to do things differently, and then he either loses interest or the changes don't give him what he wanted. But either way, I end up having to learn a new way of doing things. That takes up time I just don't have. I have more than enough to do just keeping the books without being jerked around with yet another great idea."

Hope suspected that Marci was experiencing numerous conflicting emotions: she wanted to do a good job, she was proud of how she'd been running the books, she was protective of her 'turf' partly because it was *hers*, and partly because she didn't trust others in the company to understand or appreciate the complexity of her job. Bottom line: she didn't want things messed up on her watch! Change not only threatened the continuity of her day-to-day work, but it was starting to sound as if – God forbid – Mike might actually want to become more involved in reviewing reports. And *that* meant giving him access to the books.

"I sympathize with your position, Marci. You're responsible for keeping the bookkeeping accurate, and I can share your hesitation in changing the way you do things. If it ain't broke, don't fix it, right?" Hope grinned. "Boy, I wish I had a nickel for every bookkeeper who had the same frustrations; you're certainly not alone. However, in this case, I think I can assure you of two things: first, change *is* going to happen because Mike is starting to realize that he *must* start thinking less like a contractor and more like a businessman who happens to deliver the service of building and remodeling; and second, these changes *will* involve the way you do things. You are an important part of this process, and I know Mike values your input."

Marci paused and then smiled at the compliment. Hope continued, "Now let's look at the revised Chart of Accounts and discuss how to make these changes in your accounting software."

Marci said. "Well, I already know how to make those changes, but is there anything else special I need to know?"

"I'm glad you asked," replied Hope. "First, let's make a backup of all your data; many of the changes that we will do will permanently change your file. So let's make sure we have a good copy in case we ever need to look at previous years' data." After backing up the data, Hope showed Marci how to pull up the Chart of Accounts and make the changes that she and Mike had agreed on.

As Hope prepared to leave she added, "I'm going to leave you to it. During my next visit I'm going to ask you to join Mike, Frankie, and me. Together we'll examine the company's Item List, and I definitely want your input for that." Marci appeared intent on continuing to restructure the Chart of Accounts and just nodded.

Hope left Marci and walked back to Mike's office. Mike looked up from his desk and asked, "How'd that go?"

## PROCEDURAL VS. MECHANICAL CHANGES

"Not bad," said Hope. "She's not totally on board with the changes, but I've shown her how to restructure the Chart of Accounts and as we speak she's working on getting that done. Once again, this is only a mechanical change; when we get involved with any procedural changes, that's when she may start to feel some stress. Also, I want to tell you that Marci told me that she's been asked to make changes in the past, and then nothing came of it. She's been burned more than once, and now she's reluctant to go through that again. I appreciate her candor in telling me this, and it's really important that this time you follow through. I'll do everything I can to reassure her, and it would probably help if you made a special effort to express your appreciation and confidence in her during this process. Mike, I think that about wraps up your Chart of Accounts. As we've discussed, the Chart of Accounts is the backbone of your financial system, and the way financial reports appear depends on how the Chart of Accounts is set up. As you've seen, yours wasn't providing information in a useful way. Once Marci's finished, I think you'll agree that the resulting reports will be much more valuable."

Mike was nodding but still seemed to be harboring some reservations. "I know that it's important to restructure things so the reports will look like what you've shown me in Excel, but that's not my main worry. The way this whole deal got started – the reason I contacted you, really – is that I couldn't get any information on my job costing. Everything we've done so far has been very helpful; I sure understand a *whole lot more* about financial reports. But, has this done anything to help me with job costing? Maybe I'm missing something here."

"No, you're right that in terms of job costing, fixing your Chart of Accounts won't do much for you. And that's why we're going to focus on job costing during our next appointment. We've had to lay the groundwork for the general financial stuff; now it's time to dig into the details of job costing. Getting your accounting system set up to work for you is really an art and a science. Getting your Chart of Accounts organized correctly is a science; most of the content can be applied to all construction companies. But the way you job cost is more of an art and will take a good deal of thought. What's coming next will probably be the most challenging part of our work together. Brace yourself, Mike!"

With Hope's slightly ominous warning still echoing in his ears, Mike turned and walked back to his office, glancing over at Marci's desk on his way. He was happy to see she was working intently on what Hope had asked her to do. Maybe Marci would get on board with this after all.

### *What Mike learned:*

1. *People need to understand how change will affect them.*

2. *Team members won't respond to change until they believe that it's needed.*

3. *Unless employees understand that their own success depends on the company's success, they won't necessarily get excited about ways to improve the company.*

4. *When owners get "great ideas" and impose them on their employees, the owners need to follow through to retain credibility.*

## *Self-assessment questions:*

1. *Have you ever gotten a "great idea" from a book, article, or seminar and got so much resistance that you gave up trying to make changes?*

2. *If you have implemented new ideas or practices, are they still in place or were they abandoned?*

3. *If you need to make changes to procedure, do you explain to your employees the reason for the changes, the impact it will have on them directly, and allow a forum for questions?*

4. *When was the last time you questioned or examined the way you and your company do things?*

5. *How often have new ideas required you to change the way you do things?*

6. *Have you ever avoided making changes because of employee resistance?*

# CHAPTER 9 – THE DEVIL IS IN THE DETAILS

By the time Hope arrived in the office, Mike was feeling pumped. He remembered Hope's warning that the job costing was going to be challenging, but by now he had faith in her knowledge and methods and just wanted to get going.

Hope smiled. "We'll be ready to have Frankie join us in about 10 minutes. Could you arrange to let him know that, please, Mike?"

## INVOLVE THE PROJECT MANAGER

"Now," continued Hope when Mike had finished calling Frankie, "it's time to tackle one of the more challenging parts of getting your books set up correctly: putting together your job cost categories. Since you use QuickBooks, you'll be using the Item List for job costing. But this isn't a problem specific to QuickBooks. Every contractor needs to create a list of categories for job costing. Different software calls these by different names such as items, cost codes, divisions, phases, work codes, etc. But whatever you call it, a good system allows you to segregate your job costs apart from your Chart of Accounts, to get better detail.

"If you remember, you suggested on one of my previous visits that if you added some more accounts to track different categories of work, you'd be able to get even more useful information from your P&L. At that time I told you that your standard financial reports are intended to provide general information only. There will be other avenues for getting more detailed information about specific jobs."

## ITEMS/COST CODES/PHASES ARE THE BACKBONE OF JOB COSTING

Hope explained, "When you job cost, you must use cost items. These items allow you to separate costs into different categories and compare budgeted with actual costs for a job. In QuickBooks, your only option is to use items. There's no way to access your Chart of Accounts directly from an estimate or an invoice.

"Many contractors feel that the most useful job reports are ones that compare estimated costs with actual costs. These compare what you *thought* the job would cost with what it *really* cost. This is the best way to detect the source of any slippage. If a job comes in at a lower margin than estimated, then wouldn't it be helpful to know where the overruns were?"

"Yeah, that would be great," said Mike, "especially now, since you showed me what margin I've been achieving."

"So, Mike, are you entering estimates in your software right now?"

"Why, no," said Mike, looking somewhat confused. "QuickBooks is an accounting program, and I already use a spreadsheet for doing my job estimates. I don't see any reason for putting all of that detail into QuickBooks. What's the point? Isn't that just a duplication of effort? Or are you suggesting that I should give up my spreadsheet and use QuickBooks for doing my estimates?"

At that moment, Frankie walked into the office. Smiling, Hope greeted him. "Hey, your timing couldn't be better, Frankie. Mike and I were just starting to talk about the relationship between the Excel spreadsheet your company uses for estimating, and the estimate in your accounting software."

## CREATING AN ESTIMATE IN A SPREADSHEET OR IN AN ACCOUNTING PROGRAM

She continued, "Mike was just asking whether it would be a good idea to stop using the spreadsheet and just create estimates in QuickBooks. Actually, it's a better idea to continue using the spreadsheet for estimating, but to use a summary of information from the spreadsheets to create an estimate in your accounting software. The key to understanding what parts of the spreadsheet should be brought into the accounting estimate is to look ahead at what you want to get out at the other end."

Hope looked directly at Frankie now. "Frankie, part of your job as production manager involves your reviewing how you're doing on each job, right?"

## THE PROJECT MANAGER'S ROLE IN YOUR ACCOUNTING SOFTWARE

Frankie seemed eager to talk about his role in the company. "Sure, that's part of what I do. I'm responsible for ordering and making sure materials are delivered to the job site when they're needed, and I spend a lot of time scheduling subs and keeping things moving. And then when Mike isn't around, I'm the go-to person when customers call with questions. When we get close to the end of the job, I try to check out how we did, but it's hard to get good numbers. We don't have a great system for recording change orders, the estimate is in Excel, but Marci puts the costs into QuickBooks, and I know the spreadsheets are supposed to be updated, but I just don't have time for that. There's always the next job to set up and I guess we just always assume that the last job went OK if we still get our paychecks every week!" Frankie grinned at Hope, but avoided Mike's intent stare. Mike sighed.

"So," asked Hope, "would it help if you had only one place to look at job reports?"

"Yeah, I guess so," said Frankie. "If I thought the information was up-to-date and I could talk Marci into letting me into her precious QuickBooks file to see the reports that would probably be helpful. Of course, I still may have time crunches that will prevent me from checking on a job. Maybe I could just look at it when it's done."

Hope was nodding. "Well, we're going to spend some time a little later establishing which reports should be run when. Right now it's important to talk about estimating and job costing."

## CREATING THE RIGHT COST CODE LIST

"Job cost reports are based on cost codes. In QuickBooks these are known as items," Hope began. "Items can be related to labor (such as demolition and framing), to materials (such as rough lumber and finish hardware), to subs (such as plumbing and electrical), or to anything else that you sell. Notice that all of these are the same things you have to include when you're creating an estimate in your spreadsheet. It's critical that you decide what you want to see in a job cost report, and then create an estimate in the accounting package using similar categories. For example, if you want to see total labor costs separated in a job cost report but you're estimating using unit pricing that combines both labor and materials, you're going to have problems: you'll be estimating in apples and trying to job cost in pineapples. I'm going to ask you both to write down an ideal job cost report. Think about this in terms of job costs, not in terms of estimating. Don't put in any dollars, but just list the categories that you think would be useful in terms of understanding how the job went." Hope passed Mike and Frankie pads and pencils.

Mike looked at the pad and pencil and said, "Why can't I just print out my estimate categories instead. Wouldn't that work?"

## DETERMINE THE LEVEL OF DETAIL THAT YOU NEED

Hope smiled and said, "Sorry, Mike, it would certainly be easier to just print out one of your estimates. But we're trying to look at job costing, which cannot be done at the same level of detail as estimating. I want you to start thinking from the *other* end – what do you want to see on your job cost reports?" Hope continued without a break, "I'm going to let Marci know we'll be ready for her to join us shortly," and she left the two men staring at the blank pads, deep in thought.

"Hey, Marci," said Hope enthusiastically. "How did it go with the Chart of Accounts? Any problems?"

"Nope," said Marci. "Piece of cake. I knew what to do and it didn't take that long." And she smiled.

"That's great, Marci! Those changes will go a long way toward helping Mike understand his numbers better." Hope continued, "I've given Mike and Frankie an assignment that they're working on right now." Hope gave Marci a conspiratorial grin. "I'm going to leave them alone for a little while and then could you join us in about 15 minutes? We're going to have to get through some ticklish issues, and I think it's really important that you be part of the process. In the meantime, I'd like to take a look at your worker's compensation policy, as well as your employee manual, if you have one. Could you get those for me? Also, since Frankie isn't at his desk right now, I thought I'd take a quick look at some reports."

"Sure," said Marci. "I'll get you those documents right now, and I should still have time to finish up what I'm doing before the meeting."

Hope worked quietly in Frankie's office for another 15 minutes. When she returned to Mike's office, she surveyed the situation. It seemed that Frankie was done. He was leaning back in his chair while Mike continued to write furiously. "I need more time," Mike complained. "I still think it would have been easier to just print out my spreadsheet."

## COMING TO AN AGREEMENT

"Don't worry if you haven't finished, Mike," said Hope casually. "The point is to come to an agreement about the level of detail at which this company is going to job cost. Using that information, we'll be able to determine what your cost categories should look like. Since Frankie seems to be done, let's take a look at what you've both done. Then we can see whether or not you and he are on the same page."

Frankie handed Hope a single sheet of paper. Mike reluctantly handed her four sheets.

"I'm going to make a couple of copies so we can all see your lists," said Hope.

When she returned, Frankie was saying to Mike, "Gee, you had more pages than me; I must have left out some stuff." At that moment, Marci entered the room and quietly took a seat at one end of the table.

After passing out Frankie's list (refer Figure 9-1) to Mike and Marci, Hope let them scan it briefly before asking, "Frankie, can you tell us how you came up with this list? What are you interested in learning about the job?"

| | |
|---|---|
| Estimating | Cleanup |
| Engineering | Change orders |
| Setup | Appliances |
| Dumpster | Porches and decks |
| Portable toilets | Asphalt paving |
| Water | Trusses |
| Sewer | Garage doors |
| Backfill | Hardware |
| Demolition | Manlift, cranes, and scaffolding |
| Concrete | Paint primer |
| Framing | Paint finish |
| Roofing | Flagpole |
| Plaster and drywall | Moving furniture |
| Brick and stonework | Cast-in-place concrete |
| Subs | Travel to job site |
| Doors and Windows | Garage doors |
| Siding | Light fixtures |
| Exterior trim | Mirrors |
| Interior trim | Plywood |
| Stairs | Railings |
| Closets and storage solutions | Repair work |
| Cabinetry | Central vacuum |
| Extras | Glue-lam beam |
| Walkways and driveways | Skylights |
| Landscaping | Mailbox |

**Figure 9-1 Frankie's list**

Frankie began, "Well, I suspect we don't budget enough time for setting up and cleaning up the job site, so I wanted to be sure to provide a reality check for those categories. Mike is really picky about keeping a job site clean, and I know the guys put in a lot of time. Don't get me wrong, it's one of the things that our customers love about our work, but I'm not sure that we're covering our time there. And then the rest is just the usual stuff. I'd like to know how long it takes for each of those, and maybe what the materials cost for those categories that use materials. I started out by thinking of general categories of what goes into a job, but then I remember a bunch of stuff that we've left out or gotten stuck with on past jobs, so I put them down too. I don't know…" Frankie drifted to silence with an uncertain look on his face.

"Thanks, Frankie, I can see you put a lot of thought into this." said Hope. "Now, Mike, I know you haven't finished, but I'd like to take a look at what you did get done, just so we can understand what you're interested in tracking." (Refer Figure 9-2.)

| GENERAL REQUIREMENTS | MASONRY | FINISHES |
|---|---|---|
| Architect/design fees | Brick & clay | Stucco |
| Plan prep and reproduction | Block | Lath & Plaster |
| Engineering | Glass block | Gypsum Board |
| Travel time | Stone | Ceramic Tile |
| Freight | Marble | Acoustical Treatment |
| Sales tax | Granite | Stone Flooring |
| Use tax | METALS | Wood Flooring |
| Contingency | Metal joists | Resilient Flooring |
| Bonding | Metal decking | Carpet |
| Permit cost | Sheetmetal work | Painting |
| Labor to pull permit | Metal Fabrications | Wall Coverings |
| Temp. power | Ornamental Metal | MECHANICAL |
| Temp. water | WOOD & PLASTICS | Plumbing |
| Dumpster | Rough Framing | Plumbing Fixtures |
| Portable toilet | Sub-Floor Framing | Electrical Wiring |
| Production management labor | Wall Framing | Electrical Fixtures |
| Field office & sheds | Roof Framing | HVAC |
| Mobilization allowance | Siding & Exterior Trim | SPECIALTIES |
| Equipment rental | Wood shingles - roof | Signage |
| Scaffolding rental | Wood shingles - ext walls | Louvers & Vents |
| Protection | Glued-Laminated Beam | Fireplaces & Stoves |
| SITE WORK | Truss (Prefab) | Lockers & Shelving |
| Stump removal | Finish Carpentry | Partitions |
| Excavation | Custom Casework | Bath Accessories |
| Backfill | Rough Hardware | Wardrobe/Closet Access. |
| Ditching | THERMAL & MOISTURE | |
| Road Work | Insulation | Equipment |
| Landscaping | Roofing | Appliances |
| CONCRETE | DOORS & WINDOWS | Furnishings |
| Foundation Formwork | Doors | Special construct. |
| Slab Prep | Windows | Conveying systems |
| Concrete finish | Skylights | |
| Concrete accessories | Hardware-Door & Window | Over Budget Adj |

**Figure 9-2. Mike's list**

"Gee, Mike," observed Frankie. "That's really detailed."

## USING THE LIST AS A CHECKLIST

"Well, you have to know where you're spending your money, and in my estimates I have to get even more detailed to avoid leaving things out," Mike replied.

Then speaking to Hope directly he continued, "Frankie's right. In the past, things have gotten left off the estimate and our contract wasn't detailed enough to list exclusions, and to keep the customer happy, we just ate those costs. Now we're a lot more careful about getting lots of detail into the estimate and writing up a really detailed scope of work."

"I applaud the level of detail you've included here," said Hope, "but I want to remind you that I asked you what you wanted to see in a job cost report. Do you think that it's practical to try and get this much detail? In fact, I have another client who was working on the same issue. He'd created a budget that had dollars coded to Rough Framing as well as Wall Framing. I understand that when estimating, these are different. However, his crew didn't have the same understanding of these two categories and so they just coded everything to Rough Framing, including materials and labor. The result was that the job cost report showed Rough Framing was over budget by 300% and nothing was spent on Wall Framing. Again, we need to think about it from the field perspective and what the end product looks like. With that in mind, do you think that having this much detail in your job cost report is practical and that it will help you understand how the job went?"

"Well, I've never gotten a job report out of QuickBooks, and I'm not really sure what I *can* get. I guess this would be my ideal vision of what a job cost report could give me. You're the expert; you tell me!" Mike was in unfamiliar territory here and was starting to feel a little defensive.

## PICK THE COST CATEGORIES THAT ARE RIGHT FOR YOU AND YOUR NEEDS

"I wish I could give you the 'right answer,' Mike," said Hope, "but every company is a little different in terms of what they want to see. Let's say you deliver handyman services and you average fifty jobs per week. Do you think a job cost report of this level would be useful? Would it be worth the time and effort required to track and enter a lot of detail?"

Hope noted that Mike looked thoughtful, Frankie was shaking his head, and Marci was staring intently at the detailed categories with an air of panic. "On the other hand, consider a high-end custom home contractor who might build two to three homes per year. Would that company's interest in detail differ from that of a handyman company's?"

"OK," said Mike. "I see where you're going with this. We need to figure out what level of detail we need in *this* company. And that's going to be based on the number and size of our jobs."

"And that's exactly what I'd like to have you all think about between now and our next meeting," said Hope. "Bear in mind that the purpose of job costing is to know when you are on or off budget. Too little detail will not help. For example, if all carpentry is coded to one category, you won't know until the end of the job if you're over budget. That's why we often separate out rough, finish and trim. On the other hand, I've seen companies where they had sixteen categories of trim. The detail was too much, the employees couldn't distinguish among the categories, and the information was useless. So, everybody must agree beforehand on what they need to know and what tasks belong in which category. Next time we're going to compare your existing cost categories with the new categories that you three agree on. Please think about what information *you* need and how *you* want it to be organized."

As Hope prepared to leave, she glanced back. Mike, Frankie, and Marci remained in Mike's office, silent, each staring at the printed item lists before them.

### *What Mike learned:*

1. *The purpose of a job estimate is to capture all job costs, so detail is important.*

2. *The purpose of job costing is to identify slippage, so the useful level of detail may vary from company to company.*

### *Self-assessment questions:*

1. *Do you job cost using similar categories to the estimate?*

2. *Do you try to job cost at the same level of detail as your job estimate contains?*

3. *Do you even job cost?*

# CHAPTER 10 – ITEMIZE THIS!

"So," began Mike even before Hope took her coat off. "I've been thinking about what you said, and I'm just not sure how all of these different costs can be combined into a single list. I mean, every job is different!" He paused, considering, then admitted, "I guess maybe I'm thinking in terms of too much detail, though. I'm having a problem separating the information I need for estimating from the information that would be *useful* for job costing."

"Now you're getting the idea, Mike," said Hope, nodding. "I warned you that this would be a tough issue. Just a minute while I ask Marci to print out your existing item list from QuickBooks." Then she turned to Frankie and asked how he was doing with the assignment.

Frankie grinned. "I don't do the estimating," he announced, "so I'm not hung up on trying to avoid leaving things out. I think I'd be perfectly happy to have a job cost report that had the same information I listed last time you were here. I understand what you're trying to do by making the list consistent, but I'm still not sure how to handle those job-specific things that come up. I know that in the past we've lost money on those little things we didn't include in the estimate."

## EVERYBODY NEEDS TO AGREE ON THE LIST

"OK," acknowledged Hope. "I can see that you guys have really put some thought into this. Our job today will be to get everybody to agree to what should be in the list. And one person who's critical to this process is Marci, so let's see if she can join us now."

At that moment, Marci arrived with copies of the item list she'd printed out of the company's QuickBooks file.

"Perfect timing, Marci!" Hope smiled. "We were just talking about you. So far we've looked at the importance of getting a high level of detail into the job estimate so that things aren't overlooked. And we've talked about the need to keep detail to a minimum in a job cost report in order to view the costs at a more manageable level. But there's another consideration. Marci, how do you feel about the prospect of entering job information in a different way? Instead of entering job-related costs and posting to an account, you'll be using items. Historically, you've used items only for invoicing. From now on, you'll be using items when you enter job-related costs."

"It sounds like an awful lot of work," Marci began. Her face was tense. "I'm already crunched for time, and trying to pick the right item will slow me down. Besides, I'm not a remodeler. I just enter the bills. How will I know how to code the various costs? Then if I make a mistake, I know everybody's going to dump on me. This is too much. It's stupid and unfair." Marci folded her arms and looked defiantly at Hope.

## WHAT ARE WE TRACKING?

"I agree that asking you to determine the cost categories for job-related bills is unfair, Marcie, and we're going to address that later," said Hope, "but first it's important for everybody in this room to understand what's *possible* to get vs. what's *realistic* to get. Let's see what we've got so far." Hope drew a diagram to illustrate. (Refer Figure 10-1.)

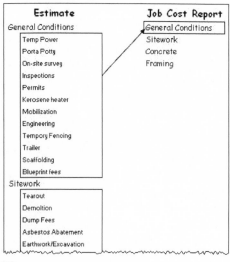

**Figure 10-1. Level of detail for estimating vs. job costing**

"We have Mike over here creating an estimate in Excel. Both he and Frankie agree that it's critical to have as much detail as possible in an estimate, so that when you sell a job, you're confident that you've based the sale price on a cost figure that's as complete as possible. So let's leave the high level detail in the estimate outside of your accounting system. Over here in your accounting system, you need to agree on what's practical to show in a job cost report. Comparing Mike's and Frankie's ideal job cost reports, it appears that Mike is thinking like an estimator. And that's very important because that's one of the hats he's wearing right now. Frankie's categories were pretty general until he started remembering things that got left out, and then he added a bunch of items to the list. So the question is, how can we arrive at an item list that will produce a useful job cost report for Mike and Frankie without making Marci's head explode?" Hope smiled at the group as she waited for a response.

This time it was Frankie who spoke up. "It seems to me that all we really need is general categories. You know, the usual framing and interior trim and roofing, that kind of stuff. Can't we just use major categories? For example, if you look at my categories – before I started listing the left out things – they're pretty much like Mike's main categories."

Now Mike was getting into his problem-solving mode and agreed with enthusiasm. "Yeah, if I was just able to know how we did on rough framing or roofing, that would be miles ahead of what we have now. I mean, in theory we were trying to match costs against the estimate, but we never really got around to figuring out whether Frankie was supposed to do it on a spreadsheet or Marci was supposed to do it in QuickBooks, and then nobody got around to looking at the report *anyway*, so we let things slide." Then he looked at Hope for confirmation. "So you're saying that we keep the detail in the estimate in Excel, but then job cost at a more general level in our accounting software, right?"

## ESTIMATES WILL ALWAYS HAVE MORE DETAIL THAN JOB COSTS

Hope was pleased that Mike really seemed to understand this point. "Yes, no matter what system you use for estimating, such as Excel or some specific estimating software package, this is a key point. Any estimate you

73

create for pricing will always be more detailed than the estimate you use for job costing. But there's a bit more to the story than that. Actually, there are four additional considerations. First of all, these main categories are pretty standard. Every builder in the country does demolition and framing and exterior trim. But exactly what do you want to know about each of these categories? For example, are you interested in separating out materials, subs and labor? If so, then you'll need to have additional items underneath the main categories. We call these subitems." Hope drew a second diagram to show how subitems might appear. (Refer Figure 10-2.) "Second, if you do want to break out different types of labor, like framing labor vs. trim labor, you'll need to create new timecards for your production workers and train them in their use. Third, you have to think about who will be responsible for coding all of the bills. Marci was right when she said she's not a contractor and can't be expected to know which job or cost category a given cost is for. So somebody else will need to code the bills before they get to Marci. That means adding this task to somebody's job description and setting up a process. Lastly, there's no point in doing all of this unless the reports are actually used, so you're going to need to establish what job cost reports to run, when to run them and who will be responsible for reviewing them."

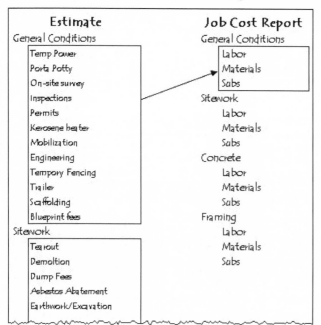

**Figure 10-2. Job costing sub-items**

This time, all three heads were nodding. "We'll discuss those matters later," said Hope. "Right now I'd like us to take a quick look at the item list you currently have in QuickBooks," and she passed out the copies. (Refer Figure 10-3.)

| | | | |
|---|---|---|---|
| Advertising | Contingency | Floor, hardwood | Project Mgmt |
| Allowance -returns | Contract Design Services | Floor, tile | Railings |
| Appliances | CONTRACT INC | Floor, vinyl | Referral Fee |
| Arborist report | Contract Extras | Fringe Bene. | Refund |
| Architecture | Debris removal | Furniture | Refuse disposal fee |
| Asbestos removal | Decks | Garage | Reimburs. Meals |
| Auger | Demolition | Glazing | Rent |
| Back fill | Deposit refund | Grading | Repairs |
| Bank Chrg | Design Review | Hardware, finish | Retaining wall |
| Barter | Discount | Hardware, rough | Roofing |
| Bd. of Fees-C | Discount-Phone | Home Inspect. | Scaffolding |
| Bill of Materials (BOM) | Docks | Hot tub maintenance | School fee |
| Bldg F-(108) | Documentation | Inspection | Frankie's Hours |
| Bldg C | Doors | Irrigation | Shipping |
| Bldg. Perm-C | Doors, garage | Landscaping | Shower door |
| BONUS FEE | Down Payment | Legal & professional | Shutters |
| BOUNCED Check | Drainage | Light fixtures | Siding |
| Brush removal | Drilling | MAN FEE | Site prep |
| Butress | Driveway | Masonry | Smith Job charges |
| Cabinet, tops | Drywall | Material buyback | Specialities |
| Cabinets | Elevators | Materials & Supplies | Story poles |
| Carpentry, finish | Johnson Cabinets | Mirrors | STUCCO |
| Carpentry, foundation | Engineering | Misc | Subcontractor |
| Carpentry, rough | Engineering Analysis | Non-Recoverable cost | Supplies |
| Cash Laborer | Exterior decorator | Office Supplies | Tear Down |
| Ceilings | Enviormental Study | Offset - Personal Costs | Tile, ceramic |
| Certificate of deposit | Equipment rental | Overhead | Tile, granite |
| Change Order 1 | Erosion control | Painting | Tile, limestone |
| C/O countertops | Estimating | Paving | Tile, marble |
| Change Order per Bob | Excavation | Payment | Tile, slate |
| Cleaning | Fences | Payment #1 | Toilet accessories |
| Cleaning & maintenance | Finance charges | Payment #2 | Travel for Projects |
| Clean-up | Fire ladder | Payment #3 | Trusses |
| Clearing | Fire Protection | Permits | Unbillable Paid Time |
| Commissions | Fireplaces | Plumbing | Utilities & telephone |
| Consulting | Floor, carpet | Profit | Water proofing |

**Figure 10-3. Mike's existing QuickBooks item list.**

"Well this is sort of weird," noted Mike. "I mean, things are all jumbled up. When we did our lists, both Frankie and I put things in chronological order. These seem to be alphabetized! I never really looked at the list before. Who set this up?"

## ALLOW THE LIST TO GROW OVER TIME, BUT WITH A PLAN

"Hey, don't look at me," said Marci defiantly. "It was mostly like this when I got here four years ago. You keep giving me categories and if something's not in the list, I have to create it. It's just grown over time. It's not *that bad*, is it?" She directed this last question at Hope.

"The good news," said Hope, "is that if you look for it, you'll see a lot of items in your existing item list that you'll probably want to keep. When an item list evolves over time instead of being based on a plan from day one, the result is usually a blend of typical major categories and unusual stuff that probably got set up in order to create a line item for one particular job's invoice. It's very much like what you get when a do-it-yourselfer decides to put on an addition. And then another addition. And then another one. Without starting with a plan, you're likely to get something pretty funky. I bet you've seen a few of those, right?" Hope looked around. Both men were smiling and nodding. "Well, your item list is your version of that do-it-yourself expansion project. And if you were to remodel one of those properties, you'd have to create an overall plan, retain whatever parts of the existing house fit the plan, demolish the rest, and add on where necessary until you ended up with something that looked good and met the owner's needs. There's no difference here."

Now that she'd cast the situation in terms of a remodeling project, the prospect of "remodeling" their item list didn't seem that intimidating, and over the next half-hour Mike, Frankie, and Marci came up with an item list that actually seemed workable.

## CREATE A LIST THAT WORKS FOR EACH PERSON AS WELL AS FOR THE COMPANY

When she was satisfied that the group had made all necessary decisions, Hope reviewed their conclusions. "You guys have made a great start towards creating a list that works for each of you as well as for the company. We won't make these changes in your file just yet because we will need to let the dust settle. I would like each of you to think about this list as we continue to work together and see if there are any changes or missing items that you think of before our next meeting. In summary, the item list will have standard main categories and most will also have subcategories to break out labor, materials, subs, and other costs. Frankie will be responsible for coding all job-related bills with the customer job and appropriate item. Marci will enter all the coded bills using these items we've agreed upon. Frankie will be responsible for reviewing all job cost reports for ongoing jobs and will report to Mike on a weekly basis. At the end of each job, Mike and Frankie will conduct a job autopsy using the job cost reports.

"That's a lot of decision-making for one day," Hope announced. "I appreciate the time and attention you've given to this. Next time, we'll look at the true cost of labor and how to use that information in your estimate. We'll also have to think about creating a workable timecard to get the labor information you want for job costing."

### *What Mike learned:*

1. *It's critical to estimate at a high level of detail so you don't "drop" things.*

2. *It's counterproductive and not practical to job cost at the same level of detail as that at which you estimate.*

3. *Finding the right level of detail can be challenging and should include those involved in using the information.*

4. *It's possible to get a lot of decisions made when the team is focused and shares the same objective.*

5. *Change usually means that members of the team will need to add to or alter the tasks they previously performed for the company.*

6. *Sometime the catalyst for change has to come from the outside.*

### *Self-assessment questions:*

1. *Have you reviewed your Item List for consistency, appropriate level of detail, and organization?*

2. *Do you depend on your bookkeeper to code job-related costs and is the information accurate?*

# CHAPTER 11 – I DON'T EVEN MAKE THAT MUCH

Hope's next visit promised to be a real eye-opener for Mike. When she arrived, Hope jumped right in and said, "OK, Mike, we're making great progress. Now it's time to look at how you estimate labor. Remember when you said that you use your billing rate in your estimates to include that extra 'fudge factor' for labor? And…"

Mike finished Hope's sentence. "Yeah, and now I know I was shooting myself in the foot with that great idea!" he said sarcastically.

## LOOK CAREFULLY AT YOUR EXTRA EMPLOYER COSTS

"Well, let's look at what it really costs when you have your employees in the field. I know you pay different hourly rates for different employees, but let's start with an average gross wage of $25 per hour. There are two types of payroll items: one that you deduct from your employee and the other that costs you more money.

"First, employee deductions have to be paid to different agencies. So, anything that you deduct from your employee won't affect your costs. For example, Federal Income Tax is money that you deduct from your employees. Let's say you pay two guys each $1000 in gross wages. If you deduct $25 of income tax from one employee and $725 from the other employee, the eventual cost will be the same. Although their net payroll checks will be $700 different, you'll eventually need to pay the deductions to the government. In other words, regardless of any deductions, you're always going to end up paying out the full amount of the gross wages: some to the employees, and some to the government." (Refer Figure 11-1.)

| Employee paycheck | Chris | Pat |
|---|---|---|
| Gross Wages | $1,000 | $1,000 |
| Income Tax Deduction | -$25 | -$725 |
| Other Deductions | -$150 | -$150 |
| **Net paycheck to employee** | $825 | $125 |
| | | |
| Net Check | $825 | $125 |
| Check to Government | $175 | $875 |
| **Total Cash Out*** | $1,000 | $1,000 |

*\* Does not include additional employer costs*

**Figure 11-1. Additional employee deductions don't save you any money.**

Hope checked in with Mike. "Does that make sense?"

"Yeah, so I'm not going to get any breaks; whatever I don't pay to an employee, I'm just going to pay to the feds, right?"

"Exactly," said Hope. "So employee deductions don't matter, but what *does* matter is the money that you have to pay above and beyond your employee's gross wages. For example, Federal Unemployment is a tax that the company pays. Then there are other taxes, such as Social Security, that apply to both the employee and the employer. Your employees have a percentage deducted from their paychecks and you match that deduction and pay it on their behalf.

"So, let's just focus on those things that you have to pay in addition to wages. Think about it like a piece of veneer plywood with multiple layers, where you start with the gross wage and then add additional costs on top. The whole sheet is what it costs your company for labor. We use the term *burden* to describe those costs above and beyond what you pay in wages. Some of these costs are percentages and others are flat costs. Let's take a look at each one."

## START WITH THE GROSS WAGE AND ADD BURDENS

Hope drew a quick diagram. (Refer Figure 11-2.) "The first layer is payroll taxes. Right now the combined Social Security and Medicare rates that the employer has to pay are 7.65%. That means that for every hundred dollars you pay your employees, you have to pay almost another $8 to Uncle Sam. And that's just part of what you need to pay to the government. You also have to pay into a State Unemployment Fund in most states, and for your company that's another 3.5% this year. The typical average burden of payroll taxes usually runs about 11% to 13% a year."

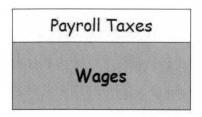

**Figure 11-2. Gross plus payroll taxes.**

Mike shook his head and said, "Yeah, I knew it was something to think about, but the numbers always seemed to be a moving target and I could never pin down the exact amounts."

Hope replied, "Your payroll service should show the exact amounts, but for our purposes, it's fine to just use averages for now."

## WORKERS' COMP IS ALSO A BURDEN ATTACHED TO PAYROLL

She continued, "We also have to look at your Workers' Compensation costs." Hope added another layer on top of the diagram she had. (Refer Figure 11-3.) "These go up and down every year, and this may change based on what type of work your employees are doing. When I was here before, I had Marci show me your policy. It appears that the average Workers' Compensation rate you pay is 18%."

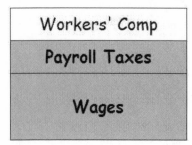

**Figure 11-3. Plus workers' comp**

"But what about that discount I get for my great safety record? I know it's something!" Mike asked.

"Yes, that's called an 'Experience Modification' factor, and yours is pretty good – it's 86%. That means that you only have to pay 86% of the typical total workers' compensation rates. However, that rate can also change each year. You've earned that discount because you've been successful at preventing accidents. But if you had an accident next year, your rate would go up. In fact, I have some clients who have had a few accidents and their experience modification rating is 121%! That means they have a 21% surcharge on all their workers' compensation fees. I recommend that you do not pass on to the customers any reduction due to your experience modification. After all, like getting a vendor discount because you pay by the 10th of the month, this is something that you earn because you have a good safety record. But you can't necessarily count on it. That is, if you lose that experience modification 'discount,' your labor cost will be underestimated. Instead, record the reduction separately as other income, sort of a management bonus for a job well done. However, if you find your rate going up and changing from being a discount into a surcharge, that should be taken into account when figuring your costs."

"So now, take your employee who gets $25 per hour, add 12% for payroll taxes and 18% for workers compensation, and we are already at $32.50 per hour."

## LIABILITY INSURANCE INCREASES AS PAYROLL INCREASES

"But we're not done yet. Next we need to consider liability insurance." (Refer Figure 11-4.)

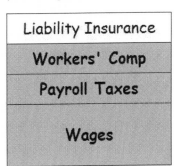

**Figure 11-4. Plus liability insurance.**

Mike said, "Wait a minute; I just had to pay a big deposit for that one. But what's that have to do with labor?"

Hope replied, "That's a good point. Many contractors don't consider their liability as a burden on top of their labor because they think of it as overhead. Liability policies are typically written as a percentage of revenue or based on gross wages. And if your revenue goes up, your wages will probably go up too. Therefore, you can say that your liability insurance is a function of your volume. Think what would happen to your liability insurance if you did five more jobs next year. If these additional jobs caused your volume to go up by 25%, did you know that your liability insurance costs would then also go up by 25%? Since liability insurance and gross wages are related to your jobs, I consider liability insurance to be a burden.

"We'll take a look at your policy later to determine the actual rate, but I know that most contractors in this area and of similar size average liability insurance between 6% and 10% of total wages. Let's just use an average of 8% for now."

Mike was thinking ahead of Hope, trying to come up with a new burdened total. "So, if I add another 8% that makes that $25-per-hour guy now cost $34.50!" (Refer Figure 11-5.)

| Gross | + | Payroll Taxes | + | Workers' Comp | + | Liability | = | Total |
|---|---|---|---|---|---|---|---|---|
| | | 12% | | 18% | | 8% | | |
| $25.00 | + | $3.00 | + | $4.50 | + | $2.00 | = | $34.50 |

**Figure 11-5. Formula showing employer costs per hour.**

"Right," Hope said. "Now let's change the way we do the math. We've looked at some of the costs that are percentage based; let's take a look at some other costs that are annual. These are costs that you have to pay, no matter how many hours a week your employee works, whether it's 20 or 60 hours in any given week. These include such benefits as health insurance, as well as vacation and holidays." Hope paused and then asked, "So, Mike, do you pay any health insurance?"

## HEALTH INSURANCE CAN BE A SIGNIFICANT BURDEN

"Well, in the past I didn't pay any health benefits, but a few years ago I figured out that I needed to pay some or all of my guys' health insurance if I wanted to keep my crew. At the time they were really happy, and it only cost me about $375 per month. But Marci just told me last week that it now costs $520 per guy! And it just keeps going up every year."

"You bet!" said Hope. "I hope you let your employees know every time those costs go up. In fact, every time you have to pay more for health insurance, it's as if your employees get a raise! If you weren't paying for it for them, they would have to pay it out of their own pocket, and they would have to make more money to cover the costs. When you pay their health insurance, they get a tax free benefit."

She continued, "A lot of employees aren't even aware of how much you are paying for their health insurance. I recommend that you set a policy that pays a flat amount for every employee, and they need to make up the difference. So if your health insurance right now is $400, you set a policy that says you'll cover the first $375. Then, if the policy goes up, you'll end up taking more out of their paycheck. They'll feel the pinch for a few weeks and then, if you want, you can raise your company contribution. This way, they know that the rates have gone up and they are reminded how much you contribute per month.

"Now, if we want to add that as a burden, we have to look at the total costs." (Refer Figure 11-6.)

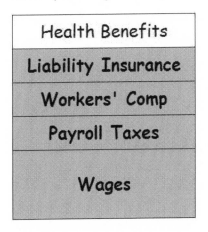

**Figure 11-6. Plus health benefits.**

Mike reached for his calculator and said, "Let me try and figure out how much it cost per hour. If we pay $400 per month, that's about $100 per week, divided by 40 hours per week, costs $2.50 per hour. I never thought of it that way before, on an hourly basis."

Hope held up her hand and said, "Mike, that's a good start, but let's look at those numbers more closely. Do your employees get paid for 40 hours every week, week after week?"

Mike thought about last winter when he wasn't able to find enough inside work for the guys. He said, "Hmmm, I remember several days last winter when I had to send the guys home early. I thought it wasn't a problem because I didn't have to pay them if they didn't work. But even though I didn't have to pay them, I still paid their medical insurance. So even if they don't work and I don't pay them, I'm still paying $2.50 per hour!"

Hope agreed. "Yeah, it doesn't seem fair, does it? In fact, the typical construction worker is paid for only about 1700 to 1800 hours per year. You can use a formula to calculate your hourly cost. (Refer Figure 11-7.) Notice that the result is about 24¢ more per hour than you thought."

| Monthly cost | | Months/Year | = | Total Annual Cost | ÷ | # Hrs Worked | = | Hourly Cost |
|---|---|---|---|---|---|---|---|---|
| $400.00 | x | 12 | = | $4,800.00 | ÷ | 1,750 | = | $2.74 |

**Figure 11-7. Calculating hourly cost for health insurance based on hours worked.**

Hope continued the discussion, "So, do you pay any vacation?"

Mike rolled his eyes and said, "Well, we didn't use to, but the guys kept saying they got vacation at their last job. And I didn't want to lose my crew. So we set up a policy that after they worked for me for a year, they earned one week. In fact, Frankie caught me when I was feeling generous and he gets two weeks a year, but he's been with me the longest."

Mike and Hope worked through some other examples of other burdens, including vacation, retirement contributions for employees, and bonuses. She reminded Mike that he needed to consider the costs involved when employees use, lose, and abuse tools. Then she even had Mike examine how much it cost when he gave the company truck to his employees to drive around from job to job and to the lumberyard. (Refer Figure 11-8.) Mike sighed and said, "Yeah, I still don't understand why they need to drive to the lumberyard three times a day!"

| Company Truck |
| Small Tools |
| Bonuses |
| Retirement |
| Vacation |
| Health Benefits |
| Liability Insurance |
| Workers' Comp |
| Payroll Taxes |
| Wages |

**Figure 11-8. Plus other burdens.**

## CONSIDER ALL THE BURDENS ATTACHED TO AN EMPLOYEE

"Well Mike, good point. Have you ever asked them why the materials aren't on the job when they need them? That's something we should discuss with Frankie. As we nail down the budget, we can turn our attention to managing the job. But for now, let's keep on track with the employee costs."

Mike asked, "Aren't we done yet? I never realized how expensive my employees were."

Hope reassured Mike. "Yes, we're almost done, but there's one more important factor to consider. We're looking at the number of hours your employees are being paid. But we should also look at the number of hours they actually work on a job. Do you pay your employees to clean up the shop? What about staff meetings? These are all considered non-productive time and need to be included in your burdened calculation. So not only do you need to look at the average number of paid hours each year, you also need to consider how many of those hours are spent *producing work* on customer jobs."

Hope and Mike spent the next few minutes coming up with a list of types of non-productive time and how many hours were spent on them in the last 12 months:

- Paid sick or personal days

- Paid holidays

- Shop cleanup

- Weekly staff meetings

- Monthly safety meetings

- Annual pig roast

- Two-day conference and trade show

- Time spent when he had the guys build the playground at his school during regular hours

- Windshield (commute/transit) time

- Paid lunches and breaks

As Hope and Mike were reviewing the list, Mike rolled his eyes. "I forgot to include that time last fall, when we were slow, I had the guys do some stuff around my mom's house."

Mike was really starting to get worried. "This sure seems like a lot of work, and I'm not even certain we've used the right numbers."

Hope said, "Yes, this can be confusing. But if we set up a spreadsheet for all these numbers, then you can be set for the time being. Then, I recommend you review it about every six months. Let's use a spreadsheet I've designed to help you through the numbers."

After they spent some more time filling in the blanks on the spreadsheet, Mike looked at the final number. He said, "Wow, so it costs $54.67 per hour for a $25/hour employee to work on a job? That's more than double what I pay him." Mike paused and looked thoughtful. "Hey, wait a minute. That's still less than the $80 per hour that I charge so I'm still doing OK, right?"

Hope reminded Mike, "Yes, it is still less than the $80 per hour, but I remember that you said you were using that $80 rate to cover profit and overhead. Perhaps you're counting that money twice. We've gone through a lot of numbers today; let's tackle that on my next visit."

### *What Mike learned:*

1. *Employees cost a lot more than he thought.*

2. *There are financial implications to giving unpaid time off.*

3. *Employees cost money even when they're not working.*

### *Self-assessment questions:*

1. *Do you know what your production workers really cost per productive hour?*

2. *Are you using a fully burdened per-hour cost when estimating?*

3. *Do you know how many non-productive hours you pay for?*

# CHAPTER 12 – THE SLUSH FUND

When Hope arrived, Mike began with, "You showed me last time how much my employees are really costing me, but my $80/hour charge-out rate still gives me some profit."

"Well, Mike, I know it seems that way," acknowledged Hope. "But let's go back to that simple estimate we did in a previous meeting and check out how your current markup system might work. Let's start with the same numbers again." (Refer Figure 12-1.)

| Cost Type | Cost |
|---|---|
| Labor (320 x $80) | $25,600 |
| Materials | $30,000 |
| Subcontractors | $30,000 |
| **Totals** | **$85,600** |

Figure 12-1. Sample job budget: labor at charge-out rate.

"Now we know from the labor burden calculations we did that your employees aren't really *costing you* $80 per hour, but for the time being, let's see how the numbers come out using your 15% and 10% markup."

Hope entered the formulas to produce a sales price for each cost, based on the 15% and 10% markup, and then calculated the markup on a dollar basis. (Refer Figure 12-2.)

| Cost Type | Cost | Markup % | Markup $ | Amount |
|---|---|---|---|---|
| Labor (320 x $80) | $25,600 | 15% + 10% | $6,784 | $32,384 |
| Materials | $30,000 | 15% + 10% | $7,950 | $37,950 |
| Subcontractors | $30,000 | 15% + 10% | $7,950 | $37,950 |
| **Totals** | $85,600 | 15% + 10% | $22,684 | $108,284 |

**Figure 12-2. Sample job estimate based on labor charge-out rate plus materials and subs' costs with 10% and 15% markup.**

## LOOK AT THE MARKUP BY COST TYPE

She continued, "Let's check out whether inflating your labor figure actually gives you a final sale price for the job that adequately covers your job costs, that job's fair share of overhead, and that job's fair share of profit. Let's change the labor cost to what you just calculated your $25/hour production employees really cost you for each productive hour of time. We came up with $54.67, so multiplying the estimated 320 hours by that figure gives us $17,494.40. So, plug that in as a labor cost. Then, remember that a few weeks ago we concluded that if you want to avoid having to increase your sales and you also want to make the target profit we discussed, you need to use a 50% markup. Applying that markup to all the line items produces this." (Refer Figure 12-3.)

| Cost Type | Cost | Markup % | Markup $ | Amount |
|---|---|---|---|---|
| Labor (320 x $54.67) | $17,494 | 50% | $8,747 | $26,242 |
| Materials | $30,000 | 50% | $15,000 | $45,000 |
| Subcontractors | $30,000 | 50% | $15,000 | $45,000 |
| **Totals** | $77,494 | 50% | $38,747 | $116,242 |

**Figure 12-3. Sample job estimate based on burdened labor costs, materials, and subs' costs with 50% markup.**

As Hope adjusted the markup, Mike noticed that the new sales price ($116,242) was about $8,000 higher than the previous example ($108.284). "Wait a minute," he exclaimed. "Are you telling me that on a job that size, the way I've been estimating means that I'm too low by $8,000? Does that mean that it's proportional? That if I had a job with twice as much labor, I'd be off by $16,000?"

"Well, it really depends on the *proportion* of labor you have in your job," explained Hope. "Let's go back to that first example and pretend that it was a labor-only job. You still estimated 320 hours, but there weren't any materials or subs. In that case, your overstated labor cost will help you out. Let's see how that works in the spreadsheet." (Refer Figure 12-4.)

| Cost Type | Cost | Markup (15+10) | Amount |
|---|---|---|---|
| Labor (320 x $80) | $25,600 | $6,784 | $32,384 |
| Materials | $0 | $0 | $0 |
| Subcontractors | $0 | $0 | $0 |
| **Totals** | $25,600 | $6,784 | $32,384 |

**Figure 12-4. Estimate for labor-only job using charge-out rate plus 15% and 10% markup.**

Then Hope created a second labor-heavy spreadsheet using the burdened rate plus a 50% markup. (Refer Figure 12-5.)

| Cost Type | Cost | Markup (50%) | Amount |
|---|---|---|---|
| Labor (320 x $54.67) | $17,494 | $8,747 | $26,242 |
| Materials | $0 | $0 | $0 |
| Subcontractors | $0 | $0 | $0 |
| **Totals** | $17,494 | $8,747 | $26,242 |

**Figure 12-5. Estimate for labor-only job using burdened labor plus 50% markup.**

It was immediately apparent to Mike that loading up his overhead and profit into labor went in Mike's favor when the job was heavy on labor. On 320 hours, the difference in the labor sale price was $6,142 ($32,384 - $26,242). "Yeah, I was pretty sure I was making out great on labor."

Hope agreed. "Yes, in fact let's see what markup you are really adding when you are using your charge-out rate with the 15% and 10% markup." Hope created another quick spreadsheet and said, "Yes, you can see that you are actually including an 85% markup on your labor." (Refer Figure 12-6.)

| Chargout | Markup (15 + 10) | Sales Price |
|----------|------------------|-------------|
| $80.00 | $101.20 | $101.20 |

| Sales Price | Burdened hourly cost | Gross Profit | Markup % | Margin % |
|-------------|----------------------|--------------|----------|----------|
| $101.20 | $54.67 | $46.53 | 85% | 46% |

**Figure 12-6. Calculating the markup on labor based on Mike's current labor pricing strategy.**

"But," Hope continued, "you'll only get that markup *if* you keep within your budgeted hours. Remember, you admitted that you used the $80 charge-out rate to cover your inability to accurately estimate hours. So, you lose some of that markup every hour you go over budget."

## CONSIDER PRICING ON LABOR HEAVY JOBS VS. SUBCONTRACT HEAVY JOBS

"And, what about jobs which have less labor? For the sake of simplicity, let's look at a job that has no labor." (Refer Figure 12-7.)

| Cost Type | Cost | Markup (15+10) | Amount |
|-----------|------|----------------|--------|
| Labor | $0 | $0 | $0 |
| Materials | $30,000 | $7,950 | $37,950 |
| Subcontractors | $30,000 | $7,950 | $37,950 |
| **Totals** | $60,000 | $15,900 | $75,900 |

| Cost Type | Cost | Markup (50%) | Amount |
|-----------|------|--------------|--------|
| Labor | $0 | $0 | $0 |
| Materials | $30,000 | $15,000 | $45,000 |
| Subcontractors | $30,000 | $15,000 | $45,000 |
| **Totals** | $60,000 | $30,000 | $90,000 |

**Figure 12-7. Estimates for zero-labor jobs with different markup strategies.**

Mike was nodding slowly as he said, "OK, you've convinced me. If I don't stick to costs and a standard markup, the amount of profit I make is really dependent on what proportion of labor to other costs I have. Labor-heavy jobs will do well, and sub- and material-heavy jobs will be really under priced." He sighed. "Well, at least that explains some unprofitable jobs we've had in the past. What worries me now is that I've got a signed contract from the Wileys, and since it is bigger, it has more subcontractors and less labor. Wow, I'm afraid my price was too low. It's one thing to go into a job thinking you've priced it right; it's another to start off *knowing* you sold it too low. Boy, that's really discouraging!"

## BUDGET FOR LABOR HOURS AS WELL AS LABOR DOLLARS

Hope nodded sympathetically. "Yes, it is. But all is not lost. We can look at how much labor costs you have in the budget. Working back, we can use your true labor costs to determine how many hours you have allowed for in the budget. If we give this information to Frankie, he can better manage the job to stick to the budgeted hours. And if it takes longer, you and he can determine whether change orders are required and price those accordingly. I'm convinced that with your new attitude and knowledge, you'll manage this job to the budget and still be able make money.

"Also, you have to think about moving forward. At least you know what your labor costs really are, and your future estimating and pricing can be based on that. You've also discovered that having a consistent markup actually simplifies things, since your pricing becomes more predictable. So now, we've discussed labor costs, job categories and cost-based pricing. Before I come back, I'd like you to start revising the Wiley estimate using the correct burdened labor costs and the new cost categories. Remember, when you revise this estimate, be sure to use the new cost categories that you and Frankie agreed upon. Then, when you start the job, and we record all the job costs, you'll be able to compare your estimated costs to your actual costs on an apples-to-apples basis. How does that sound?"

"I trust you," Mike said skeptically, "but I'll believe it when I see it."

**What Mike learned:**

1. *Estimating based on costs helps maintain a consistent pricing strategy.*

2. *When overhead and profit are covered primarily by one area of costs (such as labor), the profitability of the job will vary according to how much of that cost area the job has as a % of total job costs.*

3. *Trying to compensate for poor estimating of labor hours by increasing the charge-out rate is an unreliable strategy.*

4. *He and Frankie are going to have to really manage the Wiley job if he doesn't want to lose his shirt.*

**Self-assessment questions:**

1. *Do you apply the same markup to all types of costs (labor, materials, subs, etc.)?*

2. *Do you budget dollars and hours?*

3. *Do you find that jobs with more labor are more or less profitable?*

4. *Do you make more money with jobs that have significant subcontractor costs?*

5. *Do you know which jobs are more or less profitable?*

# CHAPTER 13 – MORE DETAIL DOESN'T MEAN MORE INFORMATION

Once Hope left, Mike got straight to work on revising his Wiley estimate. He started thinking about what Hope had said about comparing apples to apples for job costing, and he realized that he had created his original estimate so he could generate a proposal for the Wileys. Now, he was trying to re-create the estimate for job costing, so he could compare estimated costs to actual costs as the job progressed. By his next appointment with Hope, Mike had really "gotten" the idea of estimating for different purposes.

When Hope arrived, Mike jumped up from his desk with a big smile. "I've always created a proposal with line items that makes sense to the customer. I think I've figured it out. When I estimate, I need lots of detail. I gather all the information about all the costs of the materials, throw in the labor and then add the subs. Sometimes I use unit pricing, sometimes I count each piece, but I know that my estimates have lots of detail. Then, I usually summarize it to show the customer what they want to see. I know, in the past, I've given too much detail to the customer, so now I create a proposal with very few categories. But that's why my job costing was never very good and I was never able to see where I was in comparison with the estimate. What I just realized is that this doesn't work for job costing. When we originally sat down to create those cost categories, and you asked me to show what I wanted to see in a job cost report, I couldn't get past listing the categories I use in my Excel estimate. I didn't realize that they were different from what you were asking for. But *now* I understand what you meant when you recommended that I look at the end product – the job cost reports – before I created my job cost categories."

Hope nodded in agreement. "You're right! That's why we needed to create a cost category list that works for you and your company."

"Yeah, no wonder I got stuck trying to revise the Wiley estimate like you asked me to," Mike replied. "I kept getting confused by the categories."

## LESS DETAIL CAN PROVIDE MORE USEFUL REPORTS

"No problem, Mike," said Hope reassuringly. "Remember when we compared the lists created by you and Frankie and then looked at the QuickBooks item list you currently have? We started that process before, but now is the time to finalize it. I want to stress again that usually less detail is more useful and more accurate. It is always better to start with too little detail and add more than vice versa. I've seen too many companies start out with pages and pages of cost categories, only to find that the reports were never right or made any sense. Let's nail down what it is you want to track on your jobs. Some contractors have very simple categories, such as Material, Labor, Subcontractors and Other. This works fine for many small contractors, but you might want to move up to the next level. For example, you might want to distinguish among the different subcontractors – such as electrical, plumbing, etc. You also might want to distinguish among the different types of labor – such as set-up, clean-up, demolition, rough and finish."

Mike thought about it for a bit. "I always combine the materials and labor costs. So for example, framing includes the lumber as well as the hours it takes to frame."

## SEPARATE ITEMS FOR DIFFERENT COST TYPES

"That's one way of looking at it," Hope said. "But think about the following situation. What if your budget for framing is $10,000, with $4,000 for lumber and $6,000 for labor? And let's say that you go out and spend $5,000 on lumber. If the budget is combined and you want to compare actual costs to budgeted costs, you'll see that you've spent 50% of your budget. But if you haven't started the work, and only bought the materials, then you won't realize that you are already $1,000 over budget. That's why I recommend that you create separate categories for materials and labor, especially in situations where you may end up purchasing the materials before you start work on that item. Here is one case where more detail is better."

Mike thought about it. "I like the idea of breaking out the subcontractors. They make it easy for me to do that – like when my plumber sends me a proposal that separates out rough plumbing, finish plumbing and fixtures. So I should just make those same categories items, right?"

Hope cautioned Mike. "When they send you an invoice, do they split it up the same way? Or just send you a lump sum invoice."

"I'll have to check with Marci on that one."

## AGREE ON DEFINITIONS OF ITEMS

Hope continued, "I'm going to bet that they don't split their bills. But this is a really good example of having to put on the hat of the bookkeeper instead of the hat of the estimator. No matter what level of detail your estimator uses, if the bookkeeper can't code the costs to that same level, then it does you no good. If your crew doesn't have the same definitions of labor codes as you had when you created the estimate, you'll still get garbage." Hope drew another diagram. (Refer Figure 13-1.)

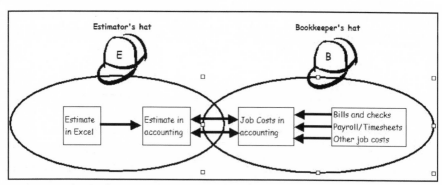

**Figure 13-1. Differing needs of the estimator and the bookkeeper.**

Over the next hour, Hope and Mike finalized the optimal cost category list, one that he could use to compare his actual costs against his estimated costs. Hope gave Mike the task of re-creating the Wiley estimate with this revised list. Mike was ready to tackle the problem, when he suddenly realized he would have a problem with the labor.

"I know we used that great spreadsheet to come up with $54.67 for the estimated labor cost of my employees. But that was based on $25.00 gross wage. I have different employees who are paid different hourly rates. Last time, after you left, I plugged in all my employees. I found that the 'burdened' cost (as you called it) was between $46.34 and $59.95. Right now, I don't know exactly who will do what on the Wiley job – so what number should I use in the estimate?"

Hope congratulated Mike for thinking ahead. "That's a really great question and many experts disagree on what dollar figure you use when you're estimating labor. Some contractors divide their production crew into a few main categories such as laborer, rough carpenter, finish carpenter. Then they use the highest rate for that type of work in their estimate. Other companies simply estimate using the highest burdened rate for all categories of labor. This second method is better because it allows you to budget your costs *and* time in case the highest-paid employee has to do the work. Besides, if somebody unexpected has to do a particular task, wouldn't you rather have budgeted too much than too little? Given the size of your company, Mike, I suggest you use the highest burdened rate. If everything goes OK, you may even have enough budgeted to make your labor the most profitable component of the job. But how many jobs have you had in which everything went perfectly?"

"Well that makes sense," Mike agreed. "But it's going to mean my estimated labor costs will be even higher. That worries me in terms of my ability to sell new jobs using these costs."

## CREATE A VIABLE ESTIMATE FOR JOB COSTING

"You're right to have concerns about sales, Mike," agreed Hope. "But we're working on creating a viable estimate to compare your costs. When it comes to pricing, we'll revisit your markup. Again, there is no good alternative to determining your correct cost and selling price. Without these changes, you would continue under pricing jobs and failing to earn the profit you want and deserve. Is your objective to keep your employees busy and sell more jobs no matter what the profit is? Or is your objective to be a successful businessman, make a reasonable profit, and stick around long enough to provide employment to your crew and continued service to your customers? I think the reason I'm here now is that you've decided that you're tired of being the former and want to become the latter."

"Yeah, that's true," agreed Mike. "So what do I do with the Wiley estimate that I already have in Excel? How can I make it so that we can use it for job costing?"

Hope replied, "Well, first, let's have you redo the estimate using your new burdened labor rate and classifying the costs based on your new items. Next you'll get a subtotal of all your anticipated costs. Then, since we already know the contract price this time, we can see what actual markup gets you to that price. That's the first step. Finally, we'll consolidate the detail and enter it into QuickBooks in summary form."

"Hmmm, it doesn't seem so hard when you explain it that way. But what happens with the next estimate? Can I still use my same Excel template or do I have to start over every time?"

## AN ESTIMATE WORKSHEET NEEDS TO INCLUDE TICKLER ITEMS

"That's a good point," exclaimed Hope. "Over the next few jobs I encourage you to rework your Excel estimate so that it contains a 'tickler list' of standard tasks or costs. Then you can link these specific tasks and costs to a *summary worksheet* containing the cost categories that feed into your accounting system. This worksheet can then be printed and given to Marci. This worksheet will be useful in so many ways. First, the summary will serve to assign each of your specific estimated tasks to one of the standard cost categories we created. Second, Marci will be able to enter that estimate into QuickBooks at the cost level for valuable job cost reporting. Third, you will be able to add a markup and sales price for each line item. Fourth, you will be able to invoice and show revenue in a way that's more meaningful to you. And finally, this will allow you to determine the profitability by line item, by budget, and by cost type." Hope drew a flow chart to show the process. (Refer Figure 13-2.)

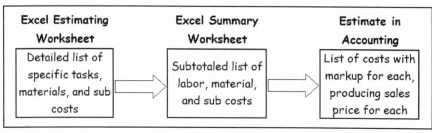

**Figure 13-2. Estimating flow chart.**

Mike smiled and said, "Wow, that seems pretty straightforward. But I'm still not sure how to do this."

"The key is the set-up and linking of your Excel workbook," Hope replied. "If you're having challenges setting this up, I'll be happy to help you with it. But basically here's what you're looking for," and she showed Mike an example of both the detailed and summary worksheets for roofing. (Refer Figure 13-3.)

### Estimating Spreadsheet

| Worksheet 1 - detail | | | Worksheet 2 - summary | |
|---|---|---|---|---|
| **Roofing** | **Cost** | | **Roofing** | **Cost** |
| labor task 1 | $ 500 | | total labor | $ 1,850 |
| materials 1 | $ 300 | | total materials | $ 1,575 |
| materials 2 | $ 750 | | total subs | $ 1,300 |
| sub 1 | $ 500 | | **Total Roofing** | **$ 4,725** |
| labor task 2 | $ 250 | | | |
| labor task 3 | $ 350 | | | |
| sub 2 | $ 800 | | | |
| materials 3 | $ 100 | | | |
| materials 4 | $ 75 | | | |
| materials 5 | $ 150 | | | |
| labor task 4 | $ 350 | | | |
| materials 6 | $ 200 | | | |
| labor task 5 | $ 400 | | | |
| **Total Roofing** | **$4,725** | | | |

**Figure 13-3. Use of linking in Excel to generate summarized costs by category.**

"And then Marci can take the information from the summary worksheet and create a QuickBooks estimate like this," and Hope added a QuickBooks estimate that matched the Excel information. (Refer Figure 13-4.) "Notice how easy it will be for Marci to enter both costs and revenue so you can track both."

| QuickBooks Estimate | | | |
|---|---|---|---|
| **Item** | **Cost** | **Markup** | **Sales Price** |
| Roofing Labor | $ 1,850 | 50% | $ 2,775 |
| Roofing Materials | $ 1,575 | 50% | $ 2,363 |
| Roofing Sub | $ 1,300 | 50% | $ 1,950 |
|  | $ 4,725 |  | $ 7,088 |

**Figure 13-4. Summarized Excel estimate as it would appear in QuickBooks.**

Mike promised to work on revising his Excel estimating template right away, and to come up with a list of questions if he got stuck. It hadn't occurred to him that he could create an estimate with lots of detail on one worksheet, and have that detail automatically summarized on another worksheet. Then the summary version could be used in his accounting software so he could really start getting some good job cost reports. The idea of having Marci enter the estimates into QuickBooks was also appealing: it freed him from having to do it, and it allowed Marci to keep control of the data entry. Also, since Marci would be entering the estimate into QuickBooks, he thought she would become more familiar with the items and might even spot something odd when she entered timecards or bills. And speaking of timecards... "How will my employees know to use these new cost categories?" Mike asked.

"Whoa," said Hope. "I'm so pleased that you're eager to get into that topic. However, we've gone over a lot of material today and you have your work cut out for you in terms of redoing the Wiley estimate. How about tackling that another time? I want you to be able to focus on the estimate for now. The timecards are a very important communication tool, and I'd like to devote a whole meeting to getting them right."

***What Mike learned:***

1. *The amount of detail you deal with depends on which "hat" you're wearing.*

2. *It's critical to have a method for estimating with a high level of detail but then convert that to a simplified "accounting-friendly" version automatically.*

3. *It's easier to add more detail later than start with too much.*

4. *QuickBooks isn't necessarily an estimating tool.*

5. *Proposals are created for the benefit of the customer, while estimates are used for job cost reporting.*

### *Self-assessment questions:*

1. *Are you trying to job cost at the same level of detail used in creating the estimate?*

2. *Do you use off-the-shelf estimating software that links with QuickBooks, and if so, how well do the results of exported estimates work for job costing?*

3. *How are you using the QuickBooks estimate: for internal job costing, for external communication with customers, or both?*

# CHAPTER 14 – AN IN-HOUSE REMODEL

"Good morning, Mike. I'd like to begin today's work with both you and Marci," Hope said at the start of their meeting. "We need to discuss the transition between using your existing cost categories and using your newly created categories. I also want you to see the fruits of all our work so far when we put the Wiley estimate into QuickBooks. Speaking of which, how did you make out recasting the numbers? Were you able to summarize your costs in a new spreadsheet using the new items list and then calculate the required markup to match the existing contract price?"

Mike grinned and pointed to his computer screen. "I've got it right here. In fact, I've been looking forward to showing it to you. I do have some questions about linking data from separate worksheets in Excel, but for this time I just manually re-entered and subtotaled stuff. I already had most of the sub costs broken out, so that was pretty easy. And the materials were sort of scattered but now, since we only have a few items for materials, it wasn't too hard to consolidate."

"That's great, Mike," said Hope. "I can probably show you some Excel shortcuts later on. But for the time being, let's see what you came up with for a markup."

## MARKUP FORMULA REVISITED

"I listed all the costs in the new format and subtotaled them. Then I played with the numbers and came up with some interesting information. Can we go over these numbers to see if I'm doing it right?"

"Sure, Mike, that sounds like a great idea."

Mike continued, "I took a look at the revised total costs. Once I had that number, I subtracted that from the total contract price. Now, I could actually see the total overhead and profit dollars that were included in this job! Then I just divided that by the costs and got a markup of 33%. I think that's really interesting. Even though I only estimated it with a 15% and 10% markup, all those hidden extra dollars in my charge-out rate really helped. Finally, I divided those same dollars by the selling price, and that showed that the margin in the estimate is really only about 25%." (Refer Figure 14-1.)

Selling price    - Total estimated costs = Markup dollars

Markup dollars ÷ Total estimated costs = Markup %

Markup dollars ÷    Selling price    = Gross margin %

**Figure 14-1. Mike's method of backing into markup and margin from estimated costs and established selling.**

"It's going to be tight, but I think I can do it!"

"OK," nodded Hope. "We already knew you'd under priced the job, so that wasn't a huge surprise. But at least it looks like you can still cover your overhead, and if you run the job well without slippage, you might have some profit. Let's get that estimate into QuickBooks. I'm looking forward to showing you how that will jumpstart your job costing process."

Marci seemed almost eager to have Hope and Mike join her at her workstation. "So are we *finally* going to get started on job costing?" she asked. "I'm ready!"

Laughing, Hope cautioned, "I'm pleased by your energy, Marci! We have a few mechanical things to get through first, and I asked Mike to join us so we're all on the same page. We're about to start using new cost categories, and that means that we have to decide what to do about your old QuickBooks items."

"Oh," Marci pursed her lips. "I'm really used to the old items. And there are several jobs that are still ongoing right now. I've already used the old items when I invoiced for those jobs. Isn't that going to be confusing?"

## WHEN TO MAKE THE SWITCH

"Good point, Marci." Hope had expected this question and was pleased to see that Marci was thinking ahead and concerned about continuity. "If your past job costing had been excellent, I'd be worried about introducing all new items and ditching the old ones. That would create garbled job cost reports with the old time, costs, and invoices using one set of items and current transactions and estimates using a different set of items. However, in your case, there were no estimates in your accounting software, you were job costing using accounts instead of items, and you only had one category of labor that you were tracking on timecards. Therefore, I don't feel that switching cold turkey from one items list to another will significantly disrupt the continuity of your job costing; frankly, you didn't have *any* job costing to speak of before. How does each of you feel about that?"

Mike didn't appear to be troubled at all. "Heck, let's just start with a clean slate," he exclaimed. "I just want to start moving *forward*."

## MOVING FORWARD WITH REVISIONS

Marci clearly had reservations. "I know now that the system we had before wasn't really working for job costing, but it seems a shame to just throw it away. Can't we keep some of it?"

"Hey, Hope, what do you think we should do?" Mike said, leaning forward. "As I already said, I just want to do it right. If the items list is part of the bad old system, I'm happy to dump it. If you told me to toss the whole file, I'd do it."

At this, Marci's face paled. "Wait a minute! Let's not throw the baby out with the bath water," she exclaimed. "There's still a lot of good information in this file. Yes, it could be better, but I don't think you have *any* idea how big a deal starting over would be! We're about one-third through the year, and if you want all that information re-entered, you can just get somebody else to do it!"

"Marci, you're right about the value of this file," said Hope soothingly. "Everything you've done to date is worthwhile. Even though it may not be very helpful for job costing, we have restructured the Chart of Accounts to separate job costs from overhead costs. We did that with your existing data, and all that historical data has allowed us to figure out your achieved gross margins. That led us to what your markup needs to be in the future. Imagine if we didn't have this good data. How would we have gotten this far? But Marci's right – what I'm suggesting is that we continue to use this data file, but that we get rid of all the old items and replace them with the new items that Mike and Frankie have agreed on."

Encouraged by Hope's support of her work so far, Marci relaxed in her chair. "Well, OK then. So what do we do with the existing items list? Just make all these items inactive?"

"Precisely," agreed Hope. "Let me show you a shortcut for doing that quickly. Then while you finish cleaning up the list, I'm going to take another look at Mike's Wiley estimate. Will you let us know when you're done, please?"

As they returned to Mike's office, Mike shook his head. "Hope, how do you think that went? Is Marci on board with these changes or is she going to keep fighting us?"

## STARTING OVER CONSIDERATIONS

"Well, remember, Mike, that file is the one thing in this office that's pretty much under Marci's control. She's proud of it, she's invested years of effort into it, and back there you just threatened to throw the whole thing away. If you have a tape measure that you've dropped one too many times off a roof and you stop trusting its accuracy, you simply throw it out and get a new one. Naturally, you'd view a bad file in a similar way – toss it and get a new one. But the challenges of starting over from scratch can be severe, and Marci is better positioned than you to see all of the implications. I don't think she was overreacting at all because I see those implications too. There are situations in which I *do* recommend starting over, but that isn't necessary in your case."

"Well, now that you've explained it, I guess I can see her point of view," acknowledged Mike. "Maybe I was a little quick suggesting we ditch everything, but I'm so anxious to get moving. I was sort of dissatisfied with the information I was getting – or not getting – from my accounting software, but I didn't really know what I was missing. Now that I do, I admit I'm feeling pretty impatient to get what I should have been getting all along."

"I can certainly understand that," nodded Hope. "And I'm pleased to see you so completely devoted to improvement. Marci will be a few minutes completing the clean up; you have a lot of items! So let's take a look at your Wiley estimate in Excel. I'd like to see how you got all of your estimating tasks assigned to your QuickBooks items."

## EVERY JOB MAY BE DIFFERENT, BUT THE ESTIMATING PROCESS ISN'T

Together they reviewed the Wiley estimate, and Hope complimented Mike on finding an item for all of his tasks. She asked him how it had felt to rework the estimate with job costing in mind. Mike admitted that while wearing his estimator's hat in the past, he'd been interested in only two things: getting all the tasks included, and describing the work in a way that made sense to the customer. Now he was looking "backwards" at the job, thinking ahead to how he'd like to see the estimate compared to his actual costs. In so doing, he'd been forced to categorize all of the tasks and make them conform to a system. The process of making seemingly different tasks conform to a single system allowed him to see that it would be possible to create an estimate template that would be flexible enough to fit any job, yet still be based on the items list. This was a new idea, as in the past Mike had created every estimate from scratch. Mike had confused the concept that every *job* was different with the concept that the estimating *process* must also be different for each job.

"As soon as Marci is done, we're going to enter your estimate for the Wiley job into QuickBooks," said Hope. "I'd like to make some suggestions about how you can create a two-worksheet estimate in Excel. On one worksheet you'll be entering all of your detail, and on the other worksheet you'll be getting costs subtotaled automatically. This second worksheet will also apply an overall markup figure to generate sales prices for each item. If you plan ahead and organize this worksheet correctly, you can print out something for Marci to transfer to your accounting software, and it'll have fewer than a couple dozen lines."

Hope showed Mike how to rearrange and categorize information on the detailed page. This made it simple to cluster and subtotal on the summary worksheet. Mike now saw clearly how sticking to basic categories keeps the estimate that goes into the accounting software simple and more valuable when it comes time to job cost.

## YOU CAN ALWAYS CHANGE THE LEVEL OF DETAIL LATER

"And remember, Mike," cautioned Hope, "if you decide later on that you really want to increase the level of detail in your job cost reports, then you'll have to rework your Excel estimate summary worksheet to match the new categories. The bottom line is that you *must* think of your estimating and job costing processes as being linked; if you change one, the other must be changed to match."

At that moment, Marci announced that she was ready for the next step. Mike gave Marci a printout of the summarized version of the Wiley estimate that he'd manually created in Excel. She began to create a QuickBooks estimate using the new items and including the cost, markup, and sales price for each line. Within minutes, the estimate was complete.

"Now let's see what we've got so far," suggested Hope. "Simply entering the estimate correctly will give you quite a lot of information. Any accounting software developed for contractors will have some sort of report that compares estimated costs with actual costs. In QuickBooks it's called the Estimates vs. Actuals Detail report. Remember how I said we need to look at the end product while creating the system? Well, let's take a look." (Refer Figure 14-2.)

## Job Estimates vs. Actuals Detail for Wiley. Chris

All Transactions

| | Est. Cost | Act. Cost | Est. Rev... | Act. Rev... |
|---|---|---|---|---|
| **Service** | | | | |
| **100 MOBILIZATION SETUP** | | | | |
| 100L Labor | 4,316.40 | 0.00 | 5,760.00 | 0.00 |
| 100M Materials | 375.00 | 0.00 | 495.00 | 0.00 |
| 100O Other | 750.00 | 0.00 | 990.00 | 0.00 |
| 100S Subs | 0.00 | 0.00 | 0.00 | 0.00 |
| Total 100 MOBILIZATION SETUP | 5,441.40 | 0.00 | 7,245.00 | 0.00 |
| | | | | |
| **Total Service** | 5,441.40 | 0.00 | 7,245.00 | 0.00 |

Figure 14-2. Job Estimates vs. Actuals Detail for the Wiley.

Mike sat silently for a few minutes. Hope was wondering what was going through his head. Then Mike looked up and, with a big grin, said, "Wow, I think this is just what I've wanted to see for years!"

### What Mike learned:

1.  *Job cost reports should start with an estimate.*

2.  *Excel is a great tool to create both detailed and summary versions of a job estimate as long as it is set up correctly.*

3.  *Marci isn't going to embrace change until she understands why it's necessary and how it will affect her.*

4.  *It's not that hard to get an estimate into QuickBooks once you have a process.*

### Self-assessment questions:

1.  *How do you enter estimates in your accounting software?*

2.  *Do the estimates in your accounting software contain costs, markup, and sales prices on a line-by-line basis?*

3.  *If you estimate with a spreadsheet, to what extent do the detailed line entries summarize into fewer categories that are better suited for job costing?*

4.  *Are you getting the job cost reports you want from your accounting software?*

# CHAPTER 15 – TIME IS MONEY

When Hope returned for her next visit, she began, "Very soon we'll start entering costs. One of the costs you have on every job is labor, so we need to look at collecting accurate information from your production workers."

Mike agreed. "Let me show you the timecards we're using now. They seem to work pretty well, and the guys are used to using them."

Mike produced a half-page timecard printed on card stock. (Refer Figure 15-1.) Hope looked it over and then asked Mike some questions.

| | | | Weekly Timecard | | | | | |
|---|---|---|---|---|---|---|---|---|
| Employee | | | | Week Ending | | | | |
| Job Name | Mon | Tues | Wed | Thurs | Fri | Sat/Sun | Totals | |
| | | | | | | | | |
| | | | | | | | | |
| | | | | | | | | |
| | | | | | | | | |
| | | | | | | | | |
| | | | | | | | | |
| | | | | | | | | |
| | | | | | | | | |
| | | | | | | | | |
| | | | | | | | | |
| | | | | | | | | |
| Total Hrs | | | | | | | | |
| Notes: | | | | | | | | |

**Figure 15-1. Mike's timecard.**

# THE ACCURACY OF A TIMECARD IS AFFECTED BY WHEN IT IS TURNED IN

Hope asked, "I notice that your timecard is for an entire week and ends on Sunday. When do you think your employees complete their timecard and when do they get paid?"

"The timecards came printed with the weekend at the end, so we figured we'd ask them to turn them in on Monday morning, and then Marci does the payroll on Tuesday. But I've heard her complain that she spends much of Monday tracking down the guys to get them to turn in the timecards. Filling out a timecard doesn't seem very important to them, except to get paid for the right number of hours. We bought these timecards so I figured everyone used the same ones. I never really thought of it in terms of getting job cost information from them; they were just filled out so we could get hours for payroll."

Hope smiled and said, "That's a really common problem. But another problem is having the timecards due on Monday morning. I don't know about you, but I can't even remember what I had for breakfast two days ago. I guess I'd have to wonder how accurate the timecards are if they're filled out in a rush on Monday morning. This means even more time to forget what you did last week. Perhaps later, we can talk more about your strategy for collecting, recording, and creating paychecks from timecards."

"But first let's look at the good points," Hope continued. "One good thing is that you have a place for the job name. I've actually worked with several companies that just collected total hours from their production workers and didn't even try to allocate those hours to jobs. So good job on getting the guys used to reporting what job they're on. However, given that you're going to be tracking labor costs by labor code from now on, it becomes particularly important to understand not only what job they were on, but what they were doing. Remember, since your job cost categories break down labor into multiple tasks like setup, demolition, rough framing, and so forth, then your production workers will have to start reporting that information as well."

"Ugh!" muttered Mike. "It took us *forever* to get them to report the job name reliably. I can't imagine the battle it will be to get them to report what they were doing, especially on a weekly basis."

## CONSIDER DAILY TIMECARDS INSTEAD OF WEEKLY TIMECARDS

"I'm glad you brought up the weekly basis part of it, Mike," said Hope. "I strongly suggest that you require timecards to be completed on a daily basis instead of a weekly basis. There are a couple of reasons for this. First of all, as I said, nobody can remember what they did a few days ago. Second, now that you're ready to make a commitment to job costing, you have to go the whole hog. You can't get your materials in there with 100% accuracy and then have only 70% accuracy for labor – your reports won't be complete. And incomplete reports are in some ways worse than no reports at all because you tend to *believe* the incomplete data and draw dangerous conclusions. Lastly, it will be easier for Frankie to review them and for Marci to enter the timecards into QuickBooks on a daily basis than to get them all on one day and hurry to enter them. And on those occasions when some worker's information is unclear, the day's work will be fresh in his mind when Marci or Frankie asks for clarification. Plus, you don't have to wait until Monday to start tracking down a week's worth of data."

"Gee, that sounds great in theory, but pretty challenging in reality," observed Mike. "The guys don't necessarily come back here every day. Depending on where the job is, where they live, whether they're using a company truck, and whether or not we have a meeting scheduled here, the guys may not even make it back to the office every night."

## CONSIDER ELECTRONIC SOLUTIONS FOR GATHERING TIME DATA

"One way around that is an electronic solution," noted Hope. "Have you looked into any of the options available for collecting timecard information via the Web?"

"I've seen ads for some of those in the trade magazines," replied Mike. "And I even saw a demo at a trade show. It looked really cool and pretty simple to use. However, we have very iffy coverage within our job area; the guys are always frustrated trying to communicate with the office because their phones may not work at all at some job sites. And given our cash flow challenges, I'd frankly prefer not to get involved with another monthly expense just now. Can't we just keep it simple for the moment? Besides, I don't want to give the production crew too much new stuff all at once."

"Those are good reasons to stick with paper for the time being," said Hope. "Why don't you think more about ways to get the information on a daily basis? You might even consider buying a cheap fax machine for each of the crew so they don't have any more excuses. Communicating your expectations and continually demanding compliance will go a long way to setting the tone of your company and getting the results you want. It's not up to Marci to spend her time chasing down the guys; it's up to them to be accountable for turning in accurate and timely timecards. But right now, let's look at what information you need to get from those timecards. You need three simple pieces of information: what job were they working on, what were they doing on that job, how long were they doing it."

## MAKE THE TIMECARD USER-FRIENDLY

She waited for Mike's agreement before continuing. "Another aspect to consider is the user-friendliness of the timecard. And I'm really talking about two things. First, how easy is the form for the field crew to use? Second, how convenient is it for an office worker to input information from the timecard into the payroll system? I've spent a lot of time talking with field personnel about timecards because many companies face challenges in getting good information from the field. Partly this is a training issue: field personnel typically believe that the most important role they play in the company is building something great. They don't think of paperwork as important except as a means of getting paid. So you will need to explain to them how the information they provide is used, why it is so important, and then convince them that they *must* provide accurate information. Not only will their information be used to see how current jobs are doing, but future estimates will be based on their productivity. Also, you may face special challenges including non-English-speaking workers or those with reading or writing disabilities."

"Yeah," acknowledged Mike. "Once we had a really good worker, and he kept asking whoever he was working with to fill out his timecard for him or else he'd just phone in his time and say he was 'with Jim' or 'my time is the same as Steve's.' The guys took it as sort of a joke until one week he had to work at a jobsite by himself, and then he finally admitted that he was dyslexic and was intimidated by paperwork. He was really embarrassed about it."

"Uh-huh," nodded Hope. "That's probably not as rare a situation as you'd think. That's why we want to make it as easy as possible for the field crew to fill out. One good idea is to make your timecard look like your payroll entry system. For example, since you use QuickBooks, let's base the look of the timecard on the QuickBooks Timesheet. This will make it easier for Marci to input information. In QuickBooks, the Timesheet has information arranged like this," and Hope showed Mike a blank printed QuickBooks Timesheet. (Refer Figure 15-2.)

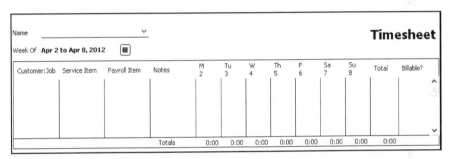

**Figure 15-2. QuickBooks Timesheet.**

"Notice that information is displayed in this order," and Hope wrote: (Refer to Figure 15-3.)

Employee → Customer → Item → Notes (optional) → Time spent

**Figure 15-3. To maximize efficiency, be sure that your paper timecards are organized in the same way as your computerized timecard data entry screen.**

"So your printed timecard should reflect this same order. Mike, do you ask your field employees to write any descriptions about the work they're doing, other than to report on problems?"

"Not really," replied Mike. "We're grateful if they tell us which job they were on," and he laughed somewhat ruefully.

"Well, I'm going to suggest that we provide a space for comments for each line item, so they can communicate something to the office. For example, they can identify non-productive time. It's important to know whether they're taking a break or running to the lumberyard for materials. They can also let Frankie know about any problems that may have come up, so Frankie can keep on top of things. The notes may become a more useful communication tool for everybody when the timecards are used on a daily instead of a weekly basis."

"Yeah, right now nobody's putting anything in the 'notes' section of our cards except doodles," laughed Mike.

## USE NUMERIC CODES (WITH DESCRIPTION PROVIDED)

"The other thing to consider is allowing workers to use a numeric code for reporting the type of labor performed. This makes thing easier for any workers with writing challenges, as well as making data entry easier back at the office. And the best part about numeric codes is that it forces the employees to categorize their work using the standard categories you've created. This way, Marci won't get a narrative of their day and have to decide how to fit that into the QuickBooks items."

Hope went on, "To use this format, you need to keep in mind two things. First, be sure to include the codes right on the timecard. If you don't, most of your production workers will either try to rely on their memory or just stick in random numbers. Second, remember the story I told about my client who was estimating using rough framing and wall framing as separate categories but didn't explain to his production workers what kinds of activities were included in each? His crew just coded everything to rough framing. So, in addition to giving them a numbered code for each cost category, you're also going to have to provide them with an explanation of what specific tasks fall under each category. This detail should be printed on the back of the timecard or else be posted at each job site. That way you reduce the likelihood of errors."

Mike rolled his eyes. "You mean I have to list every little thing that I consider falls under rough framing for example? That would be a very, very long list and that means nobody would read it."

## HELP EVERYONE UNDERSTAND WHAT TASKS ARE INCLUDED IN EACH ITEM

"It's good enough to give a general description and then list a couple of examples," Hope assured him. "Remember, you're going for accuracy and alignment. Reporting the total hours was good enough in the past. Now we're shooting for gathering data on how many hours were spent doing which tasks. If you can't find a simple way for them to report this information, you won't get accurate labor figures in your job cost reports. There's no way around that. Also, I'm glad you brought up the reality that giving your workers too much written detail is often a waste of time. Keep your instructions and descriptions simple. Also, when you introduce the new timecard, show them a completed example. I also suggest you ask them to record sample situations; you can even make sort of a competition out of it. For example, if your categories include both demolition and cleanup and the task is removing debris and putting it in the dumpster, should that be considered part of demolition or part of cleanup? It's these real-life questions that need to be covered. Then, when you are creating your estimate, you know what they consider demolition and what they consider cleanup."

"OK," said Mike. "I guess I didn't think about how the guys would view certain tasks because they weren't reporting their time. Now I see that there are lots of activities that *could be* interpreted different ways. Would gutters be part of roofing or exterior trim or drainage? I guess the crew and I need to be on the same page. But wouldn't it be easier to have lots of categories so each one could be named and described better? I would think that would be easier for the guys than having to divvy up a whole bunch of tasks into only a few categories."

"That's a good point, Mike," acknowledged Hope. "And it may be that over time you'll find it useful to have more categories. However, in my experience it's a whole lot easier to *increase* detail over time. Better to have them reporting only five or six labor categories and get used to that. If you decide later to subdivide some of those categories, you certainly can. For now I'd rather have 90% accuracy with six categories than 50% accuracy with twenty-six categories."

"I guess that makes sense. Do you have any clients that do this?" Mike asked.

## MAKE SURE YOUR TIMECARD INCLUDES A SIGNATURE LINE

"Absolutely, and they find that after a few weeks, the employees get better and better at filling out the cards. Another thing I noticed about your timecards was that they don't include a signature line. A client of mine had similar unsigned timecards and after firing an employee, the company was astonished to discover the former employee was now claiming that for the past several years his pay had been docked for lunch breaks he'd never taken. He was suing the company for unpaid time. Since the timecards weren't signed, the former employee simply claimed they were inaccurate. When the dust finally settled, my client wound up having to not only pay the former employee for all those years of 'missed' lunch breaks, but the accompanying payroll taxes *plus* the interest and finance charges on all those taxes. Add to that the cost of the legal fees, and it cost the company tens of thousands of dollars. So be sure you get signatures and dates on these cards!"

## INCLUDE A NOTES SECTION ON YOUR TIMECARD

After some more discussion including revisiting and tweaking the labor items Mike had come up with previously, Hope and Mike designed a daily timecard that included a list of the labor codes and names, and a signature line. Then they came up with more complete descriptions of the activities of each cost code to print on the back to help the field crew categorize their time. The 'notes' section was retained and a new section added for accident/injury reporting. Care was taken to create boxes large enough to write in comfortably, as Hope reported that one of the biggest complaints she heard from production workers was that the spaces on the timecard were too small to write in. They tweaked the layout until two of the timecards could be printed on a single sheet of card stock. Finally, Hope warned Mike that he should plan on making several revisions to the design as it was used, and that he should not print off 5,000 copies until he was sure the card was satisfactory. (Refer Figure 15-4.)

Employee

| Customer Job | Code | Comment | Duration |
|---|---|---|---|
|  |  |  |  |
|  |  |  |  |
|  |  |  |  |
|  |  |  |  |
|  |  |  |  |
|  |  |  |  |
|  |  |  |  |
|  |  | **Total Hours** |  |

| Code | Category |
|---|---|
| 100 | Demo |
| 200 | Framing |
| 300 | Int. Finishes |
| 400 | Ext. Finishes |
| 500 | Cleanup |
| 600 | Non-billable |
| 700 | Vacation |
| 800 | Sick |
| 900 | Holiday |

Signed                                                          Dated

**Notice: All accidents or injuries must be reported to a supervisor and documented below**

☐ I was injured today          ☐ I witnessed an injury or accident today

**Notes:**

**Report all injuries and accidents here:**

Reported To: _____

Description:

**Figure 15-4. Mike's revised timecard**

"Gee, Mike," concluded Hope. "It feels like you've made great strides! You've finalized your cost categories, including your labor codes, at least for the time being, and we put together a timecard. That's a lot of work! Now we can start reaping the benefits of this groundwork. The next step associated with labor will be to bring your production workers in and talk with them about their part in making change happen. I suggest you allow plenty of time to explain *why* you'll be asking them to report what they're doing, introduce the new timecard, work through some sample entries, and get their feedback. Order in some pizza or doughnuts and include Marci, Frankie, and whoever else might be involved in the information pipeline from the field to the office. In a few weeks, it'll be interesting to take a look at some completed timecards. In fact, as you get significant periods of time recorded – say three or four months – you'll be able to generate time-related reports that will help you analyze productivity by employee as well as hours used for various tasks."

Hope wrapped up the day. "Next time I come, I'll work with you and Marci to show you how to enter costs in your accounting software. Eventually, I want to talk with you about implementing a lead carpenter system. That will mean that key members of your production crew will actually be responsible for ordering materials, coding costs, and scheduling. This will bring the management of the project to the job site. As the production manager, Frankie will have more time to oversee production instead of getting bogged down with too many details. But for now, I suggest it will be Frankie's job to code the material and subcontractor costs, so we'll need to have him join us for the first part of the meeting. It will be fun to start seeing how all this hard work can produce great job cost reports!"

### *What Mike learned:*

1. *Getting the cost categories "right" is the key to job costing.*

2. *Any job costing related to labor relies on getting accurate information from the field.*

3. *Timecards are critical communication tools.*

4. *Timecards can be considered legal documents.*

5. *When anything new is introduced to employees, they'll be more likely to buy in if they understand the reason for the change, recognize how their actions fit into the larger picture, and receive clear instructions with real examples of how to comply.*

### *Self-assessment questions:*

1. *How do you use timecards?*

2. *How do you feel about the frequency with which timecards are being turned in?*

3. *Do you think timecards are being filled in accurately on the same day as the work is performed?*

4. *Are you tracking time in your accounting software, and if so, at what level of detail?*

5. *How confident do you feel about the accuracy of information reported from the field?*

6. *Do your timecards contain signature lines?*

7. *How well are you able to measure productivity by employee today? Can you do better?*

# CHAPTER 16 – THEORY IS GOOD, PRACTICE MAKES PERFECT

When Hope arrived, she was gratified to see *both* Marci and Mike smiling and looking enthusiastic. "Well," she began. "I'm sure that you thought we'd be ready to enter job costs the first day I came, but I hope you see that everything we've done to date has prepared us for this moment. We had to separate your overhead costs from your job-related costs, so that meant revising your Chart of Accounts. You needed to understand that your cost categories must be designed 'backwards' so that they will meet your job costing needs rather than your estimating or proposal needs. We also had to look at how to capture labor costs properly, and that meant determining what it *really* costs the company to get an hour's productive work from an employee. Finally, we had to confront the challenge of getting a high level of detail in your Excel estimate without cluttering up your accounting software, and that meant learning how to condense your Excel categories into appropriate summarized cost codes for job costing."

She paused and Mike chimed in. "Yeah, it was pretty frustrating at first because we didn't seem to be really *doing* anything, but I understand that we've been building a foundation."

## GETTING DEPENDABLE RESULTS

"Absolutely," agreed Hope. "Without understanding what was happening, it would be really easy for you to move forward making *different* mistakes, and missing the point. You can't just implement *pieces* of a system; it's all or nothing if you're looking for *dependable* results."

"I'm anxious to start using the new system," noted Marci, "because I'm

119

starting to feel like I'm getting behind. I agree it's been important to replace the old items list, but every hour that I can't be moving forward again, more paperwork comes into this office and piles up. I just hate that. It's bad enough keeping up with the daily stuff without having a backlog. I am *so* ready to get going again!"

"OK, then," laughed Hope. "Let's get to it! Remember that it's Marci's job to enter the coded costs into your accounting system, but for now, it's Frankie's job to code the slips associated with jobs. Let's get Frankie over here and decide on the best strategy for him to collect, code, and then transfer the job-related slips to Marci. We don't want any crimps in the information pipeline, so this needs to become a daily process."

## CREATING A PROCESS – USING A CODING STAMP

Frankie, Marci, and Mike had decided that because one of Marci's jobs was to open the mail, she would identify all paperwork representing job-related costs and give them directly to Frankie. If she wasn't sure whether or not a bill was related to a customer job, Marci would ask Frankie about it immediately so the bill wasn't left in limbo. Frankie would code each job-related bill within one business day of its arrival in order to keep job cost reports current and reduce any backlog for Marci. A separate in-box for coded job-related bills was created on Marci's desk. Within one business day, all bills or credit card receipts deposited there by Frankie would be entered into QuickBooks and stamped with an **Entered** stamp so there would be no confusion about whether or not a bill had been entered.

Hope also suggested that Mike consider designing a stamp for all incoming bills. The stamp would standardize the information used in coding and could be used for both job-related and overhead bills. Marci would code the overhead costs, and Mike would approve all the overhead bills together on a payables report. Data on the stamp would include a place for the cost category and customer job (for job-related costs) or expense account (for any overhead costs). There would also be a space to record who approved the expenditure, who entered it (this would be useful when Mike's company expanded to include multiple bookkeeping personnel), a space for an amount, and a place for a memo. Hope sketched out what a stamp might look like. (Refer Figure 16-1.)

120

```
APPROVED BY: _____    Date: _____
ENTERED BY: _____     Date: _____
ACCOUNT or ITEM: _____
AMOUNT _____
CLASS: _____
CUSTOMER:JOB _____
MEMO: _____
```

**Figure 16-1. Data entry stamp.**

Marci seemed excited about the idea of stamping the bills and credit card slips. "You have no idea how much time I spend trying to figure out what some of these bills are for," she exclaimed. "I *hate* taking a guess, and I *know* who will take the heat if I guess wrong, but I also hate having these pieces of paper piling up because I can't enter them into QuickBooks and then get them filed because nobody will answer my questions. Having somebody else responsible for getting these coded is just *great!* I'll know how to handle them and the time it takes me to enter things will be reduced. The overhead stuff isn't an issue for me; it's just the job costs that have been a nightmare in the past."

## TESTING THE PROCESS

Frankie started coding slips in the pile, and Hope suggested that Marci take the driver's seat at the computer. Marci took the first job-related slip that Frankie had coded, grinned at the coding information and said gleefully, "Well, look at this bill for *rough framing materials* for the *Hogan job*. No problem entering that!" and she selected the appropriate item, assigned the cost to the Hogan job, stamped the slip **Entered**, and tossed it into her 'To Be Filed' box. She repeated the process for several more lumberyard bills that Frankie had coded, then stopped when she was done with the pile.

Frankie was holding a slip and looking perplexed. "We ask the field guys *never* to include materials for different jobs on a single order or to add tools or other non-job purchases to the order, but it looks like this slip has both. I *know* that this window was for the Hogan job, but the yard slip says the order was for the Wilson job. And I also see a toilet plunger here. Oh, yeah, I remember we needed that here in the office. Enough said. That obviously doesn't belong to either job. Wouldn't that just be a maintenance cost for the company?"

"I couldn't have planned this better if I'd tried," said Hope. "This is a perfect example of how well a system can work in theory and what can happen in reality. However, there's a pretty simple way to handle this. From your point of view, the challenge is to specify what amounts on this slip should go to which jobs. It's going to be a nuisance, but you'll need to split out the costs and attribute them to the Hogan job using a job cost code item, the Wilson job using a different item, and the plunger to a maintenance and repair overhead expense account. You'll need to stamp this slip three times! If the slip is too small, then staple it to a piece of scrap paper and stamp the paper. The first stamp you'll identify with the appropriate item and the Hogan job. You'll also need to calculate the dollar amount that belongs to Hogan. Don't forget sales tax! That's why the stamp needs to have a place to enter an amount. The second stamp you'll identify with an item and the Wilson job and fill in the amount. The third stamp you'll identify with the Maintenance and Repair account, no customer job, and the amount. Get it?"

"Got it," grumbled Frankie, "but it's a pain to have to split these out."

"Yup. I agree. Then I hope you'll consider that an incentive to get after your field crew when they do something like this. You've just never had to see the results of their failure to follow the rules, and now *you're* going to see what it's like to do extra work because of it," grinned Hope.

"Yay!" crowed Marci. "Finally somebody else is going to get stuck doing extra work because people didn't follow procedure. This is going to be a *great* start on improving how we do things!"

"Well, Marci," Frankie said, "I guess I always felt you were nagging me about the coding. I never really understood why it was so important. Now, I see how hard it can be when people don't communicate or follow the rules."

## ACCURATE CODING TAKES TEAMWORK

"Great! I like the teamwork I see. So, Marci, now let's see how you handle that slip," said Hope as Frankie added the third stamp with a bang. Hope watched as Marci correctly entered the information into QuickBooks, both for the job-related costs and for the overhead cost.

Mike had been watching intently as Frankie and Marci continued to work together on the coding and entering, occasionally conferring briefly about how a particular expenditure should be handled. Now he was actually leaning back in his chair looking pleased.

"Mike, you're looking pretty relaxed," began Hope. "I have a hunch that's a new feeling for you."

"It is!" replied Mike with a satisfied grin. "In the past I've either been in the thick of things, micromanaging and driving my staff crazy, or I've been out of the office completely, doing sales and assuming that everything was going smoothly. Then when I *did* come into the office, I'd be swamped with answering all sorts of little questions. Everyone kept telling me that I was the bottleneck, but I thought this was just what it was like to own a business. But now, it's really a good feeling to know that there can be a process for things, and that my staff can solve day-to-day problems without my input (or interference). I thought we had processes before, but I think it was more about *habits* than processes. Now that I understand where the data comes from, I'll be more likely to trust reports. And I'll actually be getting current reports. And when I *am* in the office, I won't be stuck answering a thousand little questions. Maybe I'll actually have time to *look at* the reports I'm going to get."

## JOB COST SOONER RATHER THAN LATER

Frankie and Marci had stopped and were waiting to attract Hope's attention. "We're not sure about what to do with credit card slips," explained Marci. "I've always just waited for the credit card statement to come, and then split things out the best I could. But that meant that if there were job costs that were charged, they didn't get entered until the credit card statement came and I got around to processing it. Now I'm seeing that will create a delay, which could be up to five or six weeks for some costs. And that means the job cost reports won't be current. That's going to be a problem, isn't it?"

"You're absolutely right, Marci. I really like the way you're starting to see the implications of what we're doing." said Hope. "The key to having complete and up-to-date reports is to enter all your costs as they're incurred. That means entering credit card charges and credits as they come in. And *that* means training everybody to turn in credit card slips on the same day they're charged. If you're like most companies, these slips are riding around in employees' wallets, pockets, clipboards, or lying on the floor of the truck. There are several strategies for avoiding this, and the first is to limit the number of people who are authorized to use the company card. This gets into your realm, Frankie, because you've been in charge of ordering. If a job has been well planned, there shouldn't be a lot of last-minute scrambling to order forgotten materials. That means that most ordering should be done here in the office, where the charge can be entered into your accounting system immediately. We can talk later about the possible benefits of using purchase orders too, especially as you start moving towards a lead carpenter system. For now, we need to get all job costs into the accounting system, including purchases charged on vendor accounts and credit card purchases."

Marci interrupted, "But I can tell you right now that I won't get all the slips in. I'm lucky to get *anything* from the field in terms of paperwork. I'm going to bet that when the credit card statement comes in, I'll probably be missing more than half of the charges. What can we do about that?"

Hope nodded. "Your point is very well taken, Marci. You can create a process to review the charges to date online, so you can catch those missed slips early. And then you can let Frankie know right away about those 'mysterious' charges so he can identify them and assign them to the right job and cost category. "

Frankie spoke up. "I think that's a great way to keep up with charges, but I also don't want to encourage unplanned, last-minute buying on the part of the crew. I think we should consider not giving anybody except office staff permission to order stuff. This will probably create problems the first time somebody runs out of 2x4's on a job site, but if these guys are running short of materials, I need to know about it. And if I'm underestimating on materials, I need to know that too. Can't they just let me know by either phoning the office or using the Notes section of their timecards? If they have to turn them in every day, then I should be told about any upcoming materials shortages. I mean, it's not like they have a whole lift of 2x4's one minute and nothing the next; they've *got* to notice they're running short."

Mike added, "I agree with Frankie. If the job has been well planned and there's a schedule, then we should have materials dropped at the job site according to schedule. Why should we have to pay for the lost production time when somebody has to run to the lumberyard to get one more tube of caulk? I think we've gotten really sloppy. In the early days of the company, when there wasn't anybody in the office full time, everybody more or less pitched in, and we just got the job done. We tried to estimate exactly, didn't want to over purchase, and if we ran short, then somebody made a run. But now we've got full-time office staff to take care of the planning and ordering. That should free up the production guys to just do what they're supposed to do – produce work."

## LEARN MORE ABOUT THE LEAD CARPENTER SYSTEM

Hope nodded. "I'm going to encourage you to move towards a lead carpenter system, whereby key production personnel are responsible for managing their own jobs. This will include ordering. So, Frankie, you will eventually stop ordering, except for specialty items, and instead spend your time overseeing the process. However, this change won't happen overnight, and it may mean providing additional training for personnel you already have, or even adding new production employees who already are trained as lead carpenters. But until you institute a lead carpenter system, ordering and coding slips will be part of your job, Frankie.

"Right now I'd like to bring the conversation back to entering costs. Marci, do you typically enter bills as they come in or do you wait until you have a pile and enter them all at once? Or maybe you wait until you have some cash building up in the account and just write checks. How does that work?"

"Well, it's sort of all of those," admitted Marci. "First of all, unless the bill comes in the mail, I have about a 50/50 chance of getting it. For example, if the plaster sub happens to give his bill to somebody at the job site so he can save the cost of the stamp, I may or may not get that bill immediately. If I *finally* get a bill and it was dated a couple of weeks ago, I might just write a check to get it paid immediately. But if I get a bill in the mail, I will enter it as a bill right away. In terms of paying the bills, it really depends on our cash flow. When things are tight, some people have to wait. We always try to pay our subs right away because frankly we depend on them and need to stay on their good side. I usually print out our payables report and Mike tells me what to pay. That can be a problem if he's not in the office regularly or he's too busy to deal with it."

Hope nodded sympathetically. "Actually, that's pretty typical in small companies. Remember, the goal of job costing is to have all your costs current. This means recording your bills as soon as they come in, regardless of when you intend to pay them. So you should probably stick with entering bills unless there's a situation in which you need to write a check immediately, say to pay for a COD delivery."

## ACCURATE DATING OF BILLS MEAN ACCURATE JOB COSTING

"One thing that can be confusing, though, is what date to use when you enter the charge. How do you choose which date to put on a bill, Marci?"

"I usually use the date when I actually enter the bill," explained Marci. "Is that OK?"

"Let's look at what we're trying to track," replied Hope. "We want to understand what costs are incurred on a daily basis, right? Later on, when we talk about invoicing, this will become important. We're going to want to match revenue with costs for a job. So it's going to be very important from both the production manager's point of view and for maintaining accurate financials to keep up with costs. I recommend that whatever accounting program you use, you make sure that the costs belong to the accounting period in which they were incurred. For QuickBooks, you should use the date of the service because from the standpoint of the vendor, *that's the day* that you have *incurred* the cost."

Mike looked very pleased by Marci's obvious interest in implementing change. "I think we're all starting to see the bigger picture now."

Hope wrapped up the session. "This has been a great meeting. Marci has been relieved of the frustrating and time-consuming challenges of identifying job-related costs because for now that's Frankie's responsibility. Frankie has felt the pain of others' failure to follow procedure and is going to rethink the whole purchasing process. And you, Mike, are seeing that processes can free you from having to make hundreds of decisions, which by the way, means you are no longer going to be the 'bottleneck'. We've decided on how paperwork will be processed, from what slips go into whose in-boxes to what information belongs on the stamp. Finally, we've looked ahead at how your roles might change when a lead carpenter system is implemented. I think we've had a very productive meeting! Next time we're going to look more closely at purchasing and the benefits of using purchase orders."

### *What Mike learned:*

1.  *When people buy into a system, they can often work more cooperatively together since they understand how their actions affect others and vice-versa.*

2.  *Being part of system development can encourage reluctant employees to become better team players.*

3.  *When systems are in place, fewer "small" decisions need to be made by owners.*

4.  *When employees have to fix their own mistakes, they are motivated to create and work within a process.*

### *Self-assessment questions:*

1.  *To what extent do you and your employees work from habits rather than systems?*

2.  *Rate the degree of cooperation among your office or management staff.*

3.  *Are you your company's bottleneck?*

4.  *Does your company have a policy for establishing the date of costs?*

5.  *Can you think of other areas in your business where a "process stamp" would help?*

6.  *Is your Production Manager babysitting highly paid carpenters?*

# CHAPTER 17 – BUY BUY CHAOS

Hope started her next meeting with Mike, Frankie and Marci all in Mike's office. "Last time we touched on your process of purchasing materials," began Hope. "We discussed the fact that when the company was smaller, materials were ordered pretty much on an 'as-needed' basis by whomever. Over time, despite the fact that the company is larger now, with full-time office help, these practices are still in place."

## IT'S EASY TO OVER ORDER WITHOUT A PROCESS

Frankie chimed in. "Yeah, I've been thinking about this since your last visit, and I'm even *more* convinced that I need to find a way change the ordering loop. Two days ago, Al, one of my new guys, phoned me to let me know we were getting low on some 2x4's, so I placed an order for delivery yesterday morning."

"OK." Hope had a feeling there was more to this story. "You said last time that you talked to your crew and told them that you need to be kept aware of job site needs so you can be sure to have the necessary materials when they need them. It sounds like at least one of your guys bought into that new process."

"Yeah, that part of the story is fine. But then yesterday Chris, another member of the crew, left the jobsite to go pick up some more 2x4's since he didn't know about the order. You won't believe this, but the delivery truck was actually dropping off the stuff by the time Chris and his truckload of 2x4's got back to the job site. It's ridiculous. I don't know why Chris didn't know that Al had already asked me to place the order, or maybe he did know but didn't trust the materials to arrive in time, but either way the result is wasted time. Not only did we end up with a double order, but Al ended up leaving his task to help Chris move stuff *out* of

Chris's truck *back* onto the delivery truck so it could be returned. And I know Marci gets frustrated when she has to enter lots of invoices and credits. *Everybody*'s time was wasted."

Mike shook his head in disgust and fidgeted; Marci rolled her eyes. Hope just nodded. "Yup. This sounds all too typical. But the good news is that there are ways to change this process. First of all, you can simply limit *who* does the ordering. That should put an end to duplicate orders. Remember when I talked about the lead carpenter system? You might have Frankie order just the special items and anything that has a long lead-time or is not available locally. The rest is up to the lead carpenter who has time in the days between the pre-construction conference and the start of the job to order the everyday sticks and bricks. I have yet to meet two carpenters who order their materials the same way. However, I don't think you have the right staff to establish a lead carpenter system. So, for now, we need to look at another solution."

## IMPLEMENTING A PURCHASE ORDER SYSTEM

"Using purchase orders (PO's) will bring you a long way to fixing the problem. When you create a purchase order – and it might be for job materials or for overhead costs – you're recording the fact that an order has been placed. It doesn't affect your financials until you actually receive the materials or the bill for the purchase. But you are recording your commitment to spending this money."

Marci was listening intently but was clearly puzzled. "I'm not sure that will help," she said. "I mean, why not just enter the bill when the stuff comes in? Why go through the extra step of creating a purchase order first? It sounds like a lot of extra work to me."

"Well," replied Hope, "let's look at a specific example. Suppose that you need to order windows for a specific customer. Remember that you're going to change the policy so that, for the time being, only Frankie or Marci will place orders. If you also stipulate that nothing can be purchased without a purchase order, then you automatically have a tracking record. Let's say that Frankie wants to place that order. Frankie would ask Marci for a PO number. Marci can create a simple PO with the job and item. Then Frankie could place the order, and he'd have a PO number to give the supplier. Frankie, when you order things, do suppliers ever ask you for a PO number?"

"All the time. Sometimes I just give them the job name instead, or tell them we don't use PO's."

## USING YOUR VENDORS TO HELP JOB COST

"Giving them the job name is a good idea," nodded Hope. "But when it comes time to check on the status of an order, having a PO number makes things simpler. Now there's a PO already created in your accounting system that will have the critical information such as the correct job, and cost classification. And it might even include the price if Frankie already knows it. When the PO is entered into your accounting system, Frankie and Marci can access a report to see what's been ordered. This cuts down on potential duplication."

Frankie looked at Marci and said, "Yeah, but I don't have access to the accounting stuff."

Hope replied, "Good point, Frankie. As we continue to make these improvements, you'll find that you will want to be able to get information yourself without having to depend on Marci. What do you think about that, Marcie?"

"Well, I hate to let other people mess up my stuff. But if Frankie learns how to use the system, it could actually save me some time. What reports will Frankie need?"

"That's a good question," said Hope. "We'll discuss that later. Let's stick to purchase orders for now."

"OK, but I still don't see how a purchase order will help. If I have to create a purchase order and then when the bill comes in and I have to enter all the same information again, what good does that do?" Marci asked. "I see where you're reducing the chance that materials will be ordered twice, but why should it be at the expense of me entering it twice?"

"I understand your concern, Marci," acknowledged Hope. "But the beauty of this system is that when you get the bill, it will have a PO number on it. When you enter it, all that information is already there, coded to the right job and correct cost category. There's no double-entering, and you don't have to stop and ask Frankie for the information. You already have it. And, if a bill comes in with a PO number on it, then Frankie won't have to code it again. When the bill is stamped, the only thing Frankie has to do is to approve it, date it and then put 'PO' in the memo field."

"Huh. That sounds like it might help both of us a lot. Don't you think so, Marci?" asked Frankie.

"Absolutely," agreed Marcie. Hope was happy to see that the Frankie and Marci were really starting to act like a team.

## PURCHASE ORDERS CAN ALSO BE USED FOR SUBCONTRACT CONTROL

Frankie continued, "Is there any way to use PO's for subcontractors?" He was clearly interested in the whole idea of purchase orders since this was his territory.

"I'm glad you brought that up," smiled Hope. "You can use purchase orders for subcontractors as well as for materials. The advantage of this is that Marci will know from the start the total contract price, and as bills come in from the subs, she can make sure that they don't overbill you."

Hope stood up. "Marci, let me show you how to use purchase orders in QuickBooks." As Hope and Marci prepared to leave Mike's office, Hope summarized their conversation. "To recap, there are several advantages to using purchase orders. First, they offer some internal controls. If nobody can place an order without having a PO number, you'll decrease the likelihood of duplicate ordering as well as unauthorized ordering. Second, Frankie can pre-code the purchases, so Marci won't have to ask Frankie for that information when she gets the bills. And having a PO in your accounting software will allow you to track an order's history."

For the next half-hour, with Hope's guidance, Marci entered purchase orders and related bills. Once Marci was feeling confident about the purchase order function, Hope invited Mike and Frankie to check out the related financial and job cost reports.

"Today we talked about the potential value of using purchase orders," Hope said, wrapping up the meeting. "Mike mentioned that he's anxious to get purchases recorded as promptly as possible, which is important if you want to know that your financial and job cost reports are up to date. Next time we're going to address some more issues related to the dating of entries and its effect on various reports."

### *What Mike learned:*

1. *When there is no well-defined ordering process, there's lots of opportunity for wasted time, effort and money.*

2. *Purchase orders can be helpful in restricting purchases to approved costs ordered by authorized personnel.*

3. *Purchase orders can be a useful tool in the job planning process.*

### *Self-assessment questions:*

1. *Are you currently using a PO process to manage and control purchasing?*

2. *Has your company ever placed duplicate or overlapping orders?*

3. *Could your company benefit from using a PO system to manage sub costs?*

4. *How many of your vendors ask for PO numbers when orders are placed?*

5. *Who in your company should be authorized to make purchases?*

6. *How much time in the past year do you estimate has been spent by field personnel making unplanned material runs? Does it make sense to start tracking this as a job cost item so you can build a quantifiable factor into your estimating?*

# CHAPTER 18 – TIMING IS EVERYTHING

By the time Hope returned for the next visit, the new procedures seemed to be working well. With a few minor exceptions, the majority of the costs were entered correctly and in a timely way. It even seemed as if Marci and Frankie had bonded and were working well together.

Hope sat down in Mike's office and said, "OK, Mike, now let's talk about the way you look at your financial reports. While your job cost reports are looking at each job's progress to date, your Profit and Loss Statement looks at a specific time period. One of the reasons we first started working together was because you had to pay a lot of taxes and didn't know why. Your Profit and Loss Statement last year showed you made a healthy profit, and then this year it was showing a loss. This is probably one of the most difficult concepts that entrepreneurs like yourself need to understand."

## FIGURING OUT YOUR TRUE PROFIT

"The accounting process is very date sensitive," Hope continued. "Whenever you run a P&L, it's always for a given time frame, such as *12 Months Ending December 31st*. But that time frame doesn't actually match the time frame of your jobs. The accounting reports might include the first 25% of one job, all of five jobs, the last 45% of another job, and so on. So the P&L may not accurately show you how much money you really made. I always say that it would be much easier if they passed a law that said all jobs have to start after January 1st and end by December 31st."

Mike chuckled and agreed with Hope. "I'm really beginning to see why I never looked at my P&L. It always seemed so unpredictable and unreliable. And since I never really understood this stuff, I stopped looking at it. It sure does seem complicated."

Hope nodded, "Well, Mike, you're certainly not alone on that point. But I think that with the processes we put in place, I can help you use these reports to better manage your company. It's important to remember this time frame dilemma: jobs are tracked by start and end dates while the P&L reflects a standard accounting period. And these dates do not necessarily coincide. What we need to do is look at an accounting notion called the Matching Principle, in which the amount of income you show is related to the costs that you've actually incurred. This means that if the COGS on your P&L show 25% of the expected costs of a job, you should show 25% of the expected revenue and then be able to show 25% of the expected gross profit. This is the only way to make your financial statements meaningful. It's known as percentage of completion accounting, and it can only be done if you're managing your company using accrual accounting to begin with, not cash accounting. Remember, you may file your tax return on a cash basis, but you should still run your books on an accrual basis."

Mike gave Hope a quizzical look. "I'm not sure I'm getting this."

## USING A TRENDED PROFIT AND LOSS STATEMENT

Hope continued, "Well, Mike, this is the key to being able to use your financial statements to help manage your company. I ran your P&L for last year, and turned it into a Trended Profit and Loss Statement. That means that it displayed the information month by month. You can run a trended P&L by month, by quarter or even by year. I noticed that your gross margin ranged from a really good month that showed 86% to a really bad month that showed a negative 22% gross margin. Does that mean that you were really profitable one month and very unprofitable another?"

Mike didn't want to argue with Hope, but he didn't think his company had such a wide swing in profitability. "I don't know; that doesn't really seem right."

## WHAT CAUSES FLUCTUATING PROFITS

"Exactly," replied Hope. "There are two reasons for fluctuating profits. The first and probably main reason your profit changes so much each month is because you aren't following the matching principle or using percentage of completion accounting. Your bills are entered daily or weekly, but your invoices are entered on a more infrequent basis. So some jobs may have lots of expenses in one month, but since the invoice isn't entered until the following month, there is very little income to offset those costs. And in situations where you get a customer deposit, you look more profitable since you are showing income with no associated costs. The second reason your profit fluctuates is that some jobs are more profitable than others. But you can't really tell that from your financial statements because the swing in profitability is probably 90% due to the way you assign dates to your transactions and not to true profit fluctuations."

Mike took a minute to let the information sink in. "Hey, I guess that makes sense. Now I know why I never trusted my P&L. So, does this mean that it will never be correct?"

Hope smiled and tried not to laugh. "That sure would be easier. But it's not impossible to create financials that truly reflect your profit. Just like the process we created for your bills, we can develop a process to create an accurate and meaningful Profit and Loss Statement."

## ACCRUAL BASIS STATEMENTS ARE THE WAY TO GO!

"However," Hope continued, "first we need to distinguish between a cash basis P&L and an accrual P&L. We already discussed this briefly during one of my previous visits, but now it's time to dig a little deeper into the accounting behind your profit. Cash basis financials are all based on your checking account: you show income when you receive the cash and show expenses when you write the check. A lot of contractors like to see the cash basis statement because it makes more sense to them. However, when I revised your financial statement to review on an accrual basis, we learned a lot more about your company. Therefore, you should be managing and analyzing your books using the accrual method, where you show income when it's earned and expenses when they're incurred. This is the only way to judge your true profitability"

Mike nodded his head. "Yeah, my accountant went on and on about this, but I never understood his point."

Hope continued, "Well, Mike, let's see if this helps. First of all, your tax return doesn't have to match the way you analyze your books. It might be better to prepare your tax return on a cash basis, especially if your Accounts Receivable is typically more than your Accounts Payable. But I'll leave that decision up to you and your accountant.

"However, when it comes to judging how profitable your company is, you should be looking at an accrual-based financial statement. The problem with a cash-basis P&L is that you might look like you're breaking even while you're actually going out of business. If you don't have the cash to pay your bills, then you won't see the costs on your P&L because you won't be writing those checks. So, while your P&L might not show a loss, you might have a drawer full of unpaid bills.

"On the other hand, if we can create an accrual P&L based on how much money you *earn* on a job, it can show you how much profit you're *really* making. It can help you make decisions about pricing, wages, budgets and more. You need to set up a process where you can accurately measure your success and determine your true profit. The purpose of creating financial statements is *not* to prepare a tax return, apply for a bank loan, or even use in a divorce settlement. The *sole purpose* of your P&L is to manage your company for decision making and increased profitability."

## PROFIT BASED ON INVOICING CAN BE MISLEADING

Mike leaned forward as this concept intrigued him. Hope continued, "Now, let's look at an example of a job." (Refer Figure 18-1.)

|  | November | December | **This Year** | January | **Total** |
|---|---|---|---|---|---|
| Income | $45,000 | $65,000 | **$110,000** | $15,000 | **$125,000** |
| COGS | -$30,000 | -$20,000 | **-$50,000** | -$25,000 | **-$75,000** |
| Gross Profit | $15,000 | $45,000 | **$60,000** | -$10,000 | **$50,000** |
|  |  |  |  |  |  |
| Gross Margin | 33% | 69% | **55%** | -67% | **40%** |

**Figure 18-1. Results of basing the P&L on invoices instead of earnings.**

"Notice that the whole job is profitable, and results in a 40% gross margin. This wasn't a bad job; it was a pretty good one! But if you based your P&L on invoices, or worse yet, on cash receipts instead of actual earned income, you might assume at the end of the year that you were *more* profitable than you actually were. Since you invoiced the majority of the job in November and December, the P&L shows a 55% margin at year end. You might even be tempted to use the $60,000 gross profit to pay extra bonuses because everything seemed to be going so well. Then, if you look at your P&L in January, you will see a loss. You might then be sorry you paid out those bonuses. And if you do your tax return on these numbers, you'll have to pay taxes based on this false profit."

Mike's face lit up. "That's exactly what happened! And now I can see why my tax bill seemed so high when I wasn't really making a lot of money."

## USING THE PERCENT COMPLETE CALCULATIONS FOR MORE ACCURATE PROFIT

Hope was pleased that Mike was connecting the dots. She continued, "Instead of basing your P&L on your invoices, you should instead base your P&L on your *earned* income using the percent complete calculations. For example, if the job really obtains a 40% margin, then the P&L should look something like this." (Refer Figure 18-2.)

|  | November | December | **This Year** | January | **Total** |
|---|---|---|---|---|---|
| Income | $45,000 | $65,000 | **$110,000** | $15,000 | **$125,000** |
| WIP Adjustment | $3,000 | -$19,000 | **-$16,000** | $16,000 | **$0** |
| COGS | -$30,000 | -$20,000 | **-$50,000** | -$25,000 | **-$75,000** |
| Gross Profit | $18,000 | $26,000 | **$44,000** | $6,000 | **$50,000** |
|  |  |  |  |  |  |
| Gross Margin | 40% | 40% | **40%** | 40% | **40%** |

**Figure 18-2. Results of using a WIP adjustment to create a P&L based on earnings.**

"Notice that the Gross Margin is consistent across all months, due to the adjustment. This adjustment is called a Work In Progress (WIP) Adjustment. It is calculated each month to adjust your P&L from *invoiced* amounts to *earned* amounts. So, if you've completed 25% of a job, then you can only show 25% of the contract price as income on your P&L, no matter how much you've really invoiced or received. If your P&L shows more than 25% of the contract price, this would be called *overbilling*. That means that you have invoiced more than – or *over* – the amount that you actually earned. And if you're showing less than 25% of the contract price as income, this would be called *underbilling*, which means that you have invoiced less than – or *under* – the amount that you have earned. The WIP adjustment corrects this so your P&L shows how much you've really earned. Overbillings and underbillings will also show on your Balance Sheet. Overbillings are considered a liability, and underbillings are considered an asset. After you make this adjustment, you can quickly see how much of the money that you've invoiced doesn't belong to you (overbillings), or how much you've really earned but haven't invoiced yet (underbillings).

"We'll discuss the formula for WIP on our next visit, but I want you to think about how you want to use your P&L to manage your business."

### *What Mike learned:*

1.  *While a cash-basis tax return might appear easier to read, it doesn't tell you what you need to know to make strategic financial decisions.*

2.  *WIP means Work in Progress and is used to adjust your income so that it represents what you actually <u>earned</u> on the job as opposed to how much cash you did or didn't collect.*

3.  *The tax return can be prepared on a cash basis, but to run a company, you should look at accrual-based financial statements.*

4.  *The information that an accurate P&L provides can really help you make decisions and manage your company.*

### *Self-assessment questions:*

1.  *To what extent are you adjusting revenue to match costs?*

2.  *Are you running your financial reports on a cash or accrual basis?*

3.  *Do constant swings in reported profitability have you confused and/or cause a lack of confidence in the performance of your business?*

4.  *Do you wish you'd taken accounting classes before you started your own business? Should you look into courses like business*

*management, financial management, business accounting, or job costing?*

5. *Is it time to obtain a professional construction certification?*

6. *Are you asking your accountant the right questions, and are you getting answers that you understand?*

# CHAPTER 19 – WIP OR RIP

When Hope arrived for her next visit, Mike was buried in paper. He looked up from his desk in confusion. "Boy, I started looking over my financial statements for the last few years. I even had Marci print out that trended P&L that you recommended. I noticed that after we made those changes to the chart of accounts, I can actually see my gross profit. Marci even showed me how I could print out a trended P&L with both the gross profit and the gross margin. Now, I can see that my gross margin is all over the map! Is that a good thing or a bad thing?"

Hope smiled and congratulated Mike on doing his research. "I can see how you've been using the information from our last meeting to try and get a handle on your numbers. You have the same problem that most contractors have: a gross margin that is based on when you sent invoices, not when you earned the income. What we need to do is look at your Profit and Loss Statements and enter an adjustment to make the numbers more meaningful."

## GETTING MEANINGFUL NUMBERS

Hope continued, "Remember how I said that we need to revise your statement to utilize the percentage of completion method of recognizing income? I also called it the Matching Principle. Let's look at the formula for the WIP adjustment." (Refer Figure 19-1.)

$$\frac{\text{Cost to Date}}{\text{Estimated Costs}} = \text{\% Complete} \times \text{Contract Price} = \text{Earnings} - \text{Billings} = \frac{\text{(Over)/Under}}{\text{Billings}}$$

**Figure 19-1. Percentage completion formula for WIP calculations.**

"Notice that we first have to determine the percentage of completion on any given job. And the way to do that is to take the costs to date including change order costs and divide by the total estimated costs, including costs of change orders items and known slippage dollars to date. That will give you the percentage of the costs that you've spent, or, to put it another way, your *percent complete* on the job. Then we can use that percentage to determine how much of the income from the job you can show on your P&L. If you take the percent complete times the current contract amount, including the original contract and the sales price of approved change orders, you'll see how much money you've earned on the job. Now you know the number that you need to show on your P&L. Then we compare that number to the amount of money that you've invoiced the customer for, and you can see if you are overbilled or underbilled."

"Whew," said Mike. "That's a lot of math. I'm not sure I follow you."

## THE WIP FORMULA BROKEN DOWN INTO STEPS

"OK, Mike, take a deep breath. I know that sounds really complicated, but we're going to go through it one step at a time. Let's use the following numbers as an example. You have a job that you estimated to cost $140,000, and you sold the job for $203,000. That means the job should produce a gross profit of $63,000. Can you tell me what the expected margin is on this job?"

Mike said, "Wait a minute. I *know* how to figure *this* out!" Mike pulled out his small calculator and punched in some numbers. "If I take $63,000 and divide by $203,000 I get 31%. That means the job is priced to produce a 31% gross margin! Ta-daa!" Mike said, giving Hope a high five. Then he paused and looked a bit worried. "I'm right, aren't I?" he asked. (Refer Figure 19-2.)

| Gross Profit | | Contract Price | | Margin % |
|---|---|---|---|---|
| $63,000 | ÷ | $203,000 | = | 31% |

Figure 19-2. Calculating Gross Margin on sample job.

## DETERMINE YOUR PERCENT COMPLETE

Hope smiled, "Yes, you're absolutely correct. Now, let's say that you've spent $49,000 so far on the job. What percent complete are you?"

Mike punched some more numbers on his calculator. "That's easy. If I spent $49,000 and had a total job budget of $140,000, that means I'm 35% complete." (Refer Figure 19-3.)

| Cost to date | | Estimated costs | | % Complete |
|---|---|---|---|---|
| $49,000 | ÷ | $140,000 | = | 35% |

Figure 19-3. Calculating percent complete on sample job.

"Right!" said Hope. "OK, those were the easy ones. Now, how much total income can you say that you've *earned* on the job?"

## DETERMINE YOUR ACTUAL EARNINGS

Mike wasn't as sure of himself as before, but he talked himself through it. "Well, if the job is 35% complete, and the contract price was $203,000, then that means I need to show 35% of the contract price. That means I've earned $71,050 in income." (Refer Figure 19-4.)

| % Complete | | Contract Price | | Earnings |
|---|---|---|---|---|
| 35% | x | $203,000 | = | $71,050 |

Figure 19-4. Calculating earnings on sample job.

"Right again!" said Hope. "In fact, let's test that out. If you've earned $71,050 and spent $49,000, then you have earned a gross profit of $22,050 so far. And if you take $22,050 and divide by $71,050, you again get that same 31% margin." (Refer Figure 19-5.)

| Earnings | Cost | Earned Gross Profit |
|----------|------|---------------------|
| $71,050 | - $49,000 = | $22,050 |
| | | |
| Earned Gross Profit | Earnings | Margin % |
| $22,050 | ÷ $71,050 = | 31% |

**Figure 19-5. Calculating earned gross profit sample job**

"OK," said Mike. "I think I'm getting this."

## DETERMINE IF YOU ARE OVERBILLED OR UNDERBILLED

Hope continued, "Now the real question is what have you billed the customer? If you've invoiced the customer for $90,000, then you're overbilled on the job because we've just figured out that you've invoiced more than you earned."

"Overbilled? Does that mean I would need to give money back to the customer?"

"Certainly not!" said Hope with a smile. "But it *does* mean that you've overstated your income on your P&L by the difference between what you've *earned* and what you've *invoiced*. You'll need to reduce your income by that difference. Let's see what that number would be." (Refer Figure 19-6)

| Earnings | Billings (Invoiced) | (Over)/Under Billings |
|----------|---------------------|------------------------|
| $71,050 | - $90,000 | = ($18,950) |

**Figure 19-6. Calculating overbillings or underbillings.**

Hope pointed to the $18,950 figure and continued, "If we subtract the amount that you've invoiced on the job from the amount that you can really say that you earned, you can see that you are about $19,000 overbilled on the job. That means if you were to create a P&L statement that includes this fictitious job, you'd be overstating your income on your P&L by about $19,000, which in turn means that your gross profit *and* your net profit would also be about $19,000 too high."

143

"Hmmm," muttered Mike. "That's a lot of formulas!"

"Yes, I agree, but let's see if it helps if I put all the math into just one formula," smiled Hope as she wrote down the entire formula. (Refer Figure 19-7)

$$\frac{\text{Cost to Date}}{\text{Estimated Costs}} = \%\text{ Complete} \times \text{Contract Price} = \text{Earnings} - \text{Billings} = \frac{(\text{Over})/\text{Under}}{\text{Billings}}$$

$$\frac{\$49,000}{\$140,000} = 35\% \times \$203,000 = \$71,050 - \$90,000 = (\$18,950)$$

**Figure 19-7. Percentage completion formula for WIP calculations for sample job.**

She continued, "Notice that if you're overbilled, the excess will be shown as a *negative* figure in the (Over)/Under column. That's because you need to *subtract* these dollars from income in order to show only what you've earned. If you are underbilled, you'd have to *add* more to get the right income figure, so the (Over)/Under column would show a *positive* number."

Mike looked over the spreadsheet that Hope had brought with her. He looked up with a smile and said, "Wow, I hate to sound like a broken record, but this is the first time this stuff has started to make any sense. I can see that if I finished the year with this overbilling amount, then I'm fooling myself into thinking I've made more money than I really have. And I've also set myself up for failure in the following months because there won't be enough income to show a profit. I've used up too much profit in the first third of the job."

Hope smiled and congratulated Mike on his understanding of the consequences of overbillings. "Now remember, overbillings can actually help cash flow. The sooner you get your customer's money, the easier it is to pay for your customer's costs. So, overbillings can be good for a company. It's just that you need to know *how much* you are overbilled, so you don't spend that money for other jobs, a new truck or even bonuses based on false profits."

## WHAT IF YOU ARE UNDERBILLED?

"On the other hand, let's look at the opposite of overbillings. Suppose, in the same example, you've only invoiced the customer $50,000. What would that mean?"

Mike thought about it for a minute. He asked Hope, "Aren't the numbers almost the same? Can't I still show earnings of $71,050?"

"Yes, absolutely! But, now your P&L only shows income of $50,000, so we would need to adjust your income up. This is because instead of being *overbilled*, you are now *underbilled* on the job. Do you know by how much?"

Mike almost jumped over the desk to answer quickly. "Yes, I'm $21,050 underbilled." (Refer Figure 19-8.)

| Earnings | | Billings/ Invoices | | (Over)/Under Billings |
|----------|---|----------|---|----------|
| $71,050 | - | $50,000 | = | $21,050 |

Figure 19-8. Calculating over or under billings.

## ADJUST YOUR P&L

Hope agreed. "Right! So, let's look at it another way. Let's compare the two examples." (Refer Figure 19-9.) "Notice that after the WIP adjustment, the gross profit is the same and the gross margin is the same as well.

| | Adjust for Overbilling | Adjust for Underbilling |
|---|---|---|
| Invoiced | $90,000 | $50,000 |
| WIP Adjustment | -$18,950 | $21,050 |
| Total Income | $71,050 | $71,050 |
| COGS | -$49,000 | -$49,000 |
| Gross Profit | $22,050 | $22,050 |
| Gross Margin | 31% | 31% |

Figure 19-9. Comparing P&L after adjustment for over or under billings.

"What this means is that you are using your costs to date to determine how much income you can show. But these numbers will tell the truth *only* if the job is on track. If you're running over budget and don't adjust your total estimated costs accordingly, then you will appear to have a higher percentage of completion than you really do. That means that you will recognize more income than you should. At the end of the job when all the costs are in, you won't have any income left to match to the costs. Then, your achieved gross margin will suddenly appear to drop. That's why it's important to review the monthly WIP adjustments to make sure the percent complete figures matches reality."

Mike thought about this for a minute. "OK, I get this, but I'm still not sure how I'm going to use this information in my business."

"That's a great question," Hope replied. "This is a process that you need to go through to produce a *management P&L* that will help you run your business, make informed decisions, and improve profitability. It has nothing to do with your tax return. Since you file your returns on a cash basis, your accountant will probably not include this adjustment, but that doesn't mean you don't need to do it. I'll work with Marci to develop a WIP adjustment spreadsheet so we can review your numbers at the end of each month. In fact, since we'll now be getting estimates into your accounting system as well as accurate job costing reports, I can show Marci how to get this information out of QuickBooks. We will create a process where she can produce the WIP report and go over the numbers with you. I'll teach her how to make the monthly WIP adjustment so that you can now get accurate P&L statements. Does that sound good?"

Mike said, "Yup! I knew we were on the right track. I'm looking forward to really getting some numbers that will help me manage this business."

"Good!" said Hope. "Then the next step is to discuss invoicing. We've spent a lot of time making sure your job costs are entered correctly, so the next step is to look at your income. And that means we need to look at invoices."

### What Mike learned:

1. *Without adjusting your books for overbillings or underbillings, you can't use your P&L numbers to manage your business accurately.*

2. It's possible to use your accounting software to generate a report that will help you calculate the proper WIP adjustments

3. Overbillings are good for cash flow, but if you don't know how much you're overbilled, you can get yourself into big trouble if you assume the money is profit.

4. WIP adjustments are only as good as your budget figures; if you don't adjust for being over budget, your numbers will look too good to be true – and they will be!

5. Effective WIP adjustments depend on everybody's accurate and timely input.

### Self-assessment questions:

1. Do you know if, when and by how much you are under- or overbilled on each job?

2. Have you ever had a job that looked profitable until the end, when you ran out of money?

3. Have you ever made a major purchase with money you thought was profit only to discover later that you needed those dollars to pay for additional job costs?

# CHAPTER 20 – IF YOU DON'T ASK, YOU WON'T RECEIVE

Hope met with Mike and Marci in Mike's office. She began, "In the past, you weren't entering estimates into your account system. One of the results of this was that you were never able to compare estimated costs to actual costs. But another result is that you were unable to create invoices directly from estimates. Most construction accounting systems will let you do this; in fact, QuickBooks does it very well.

## WHAT'S IN YOUR INVOICE?

Marci looked intrigued and spoke up suddenly. "For fixed price jobs I usually create an invoice with one line item called 'Payment' because it's easy for the customers to understand, and it's fast for me to do. But on some jobs, Mike has asked me to itemize the invoice because the customers wanted to see what they were paying for. Since it was a contract price *anyway* this didn't make a lot of sense to me, but I just tried to give Mike what he wanted. The problem was that it was really time-consuming to try to figure out what to put into the invoice so that the bottom line matched the payment schedule amount and still have the line items make sense. Frankly, most of the time I just fudged the numbers to make the total come out right."

"Gee, I guess I never really saw it from your point of view." Mike shrugged. "Now I can see that might be hard to do." Then he turned to Hope. "What do *you* think we should put on an invoice for a fixed price job?"

"That's a common question," said Hope, "and it's something that most companies grapple with. Let me ask you this. Let's say you buy a truck and take out a loan to cover the purchase price. When you get your coupon book, do you expect each payment coupon to list what parts of the truck you're paying for? I mean, does coupon #1 say 'front tires and driver's air bag' while coupon #2 says 'steering wheel and CD player'? Of course not! So I often wonder why, when contractors sell a job for a fixed price, they often feel compelled to explain exactly what each payment covers. Why is that, Mike?"

## HAVE A STANDARD POLICY FOR WHAT INVOICES CONTAIN

"Well," said Mike slowly, "to be honest, I'm not sure. I think sometimes I feel like I want to tell them what we've gotten done on the job, to sort of justify what we're charging. On other occasions we've had a fussy customer who insisted on having detailed invoices, and we simply knuckled under to them. Like everything else, we invoiced based on habit and in response to somebody else's demands. We really didn't have a policy – we still don't – and the results prove it."

Marci muttered something under her breath and Hope turned to her. "Is there some insight you can add, Marci?"

Avoiding Mike's gaze, Marci paused, looking uncomfortable. "Well, I just think there are too many times when people in this company are asked to change the way they do things, or provide extra information or research stuff for customers: things the customer is not even paying for or being charged for. Stuff that's frankly none of their business. It feels like a big waste of time and what's the point? Even if I *do* come up with a complete list of bills or charge slips for a particular job because some anal-retentive nutcase customer wants to see it, I'm sure they never even look at it. Or if they do, they pick it apart, and then Mike makes me give them a credit because they're whining. Sometimes, I think I should try whining myself!"

There was a moment's silence during which Hope wondered which way this would go. Finally Mike snorted, stifling a laugh and Marci glared at him. Then after a moment she too began to laugh. Within moments both Mike and Marci were convulsed with laughter. Marci finally wiped her eyes and admitted, "Wow, I've wanted to say that for a really long time. I have to say it felt good to get it out."

"Hey, Marci, why don't you tell me how you *really* feel," said Mike with a grin. "But I have to admit you're right – I sometimes let customers walk all over me and the quickest way to shut them up was to give them what they wanted. So now that that's out in the open, Hope, what do you suggest?"

## HOW MUCH INFORMATION DOES THE CUSTOMER NEED TO SEE?

Hope was *extremely* relieved that Marci's criticism had made Mike think instead of react defensively. "First of all, when we're talking about contract price jobs, everybody needs to understand that the price is the price. Once your customers sign the contract, they have no reason to complain as long as you continue to provide the work outlined and ask for money according to the payment schedule. When they sign, they are agreeing to several things: first, the scope of work to be performed; second, the price of that work; third, the number and amounts of payments. So, whether you divide the job into regular installments or create milestone invoices based on phases, there's no reason to provide additional details about what's covered in each invoice. The goal is to invoice as much as possible, as soon as possible, to be sure you're paying for job costs using the customer's money instead of your own. Actually, any time you're not using customers' money to pay for their job costs, you're essentially providing them with an interest-free loan! So forget about trying to defend why you're asking them for money. Explain the basis of your payment schedule *before they sign the contract* so they understand the logic behind how the payments are structured. But the only things you *need* to have on an invoice is a simple description such as 'payment #2 of 5' or 'payment at delivery of drywall' and the amount. That's it!"

Mike was taking it all in, but still seemed to cling to the old ways. "But," he protested, "what do you do when a customer is insistent about how they want to see things done?"

## WHO'S RUNNING THE JOB?

"Tail wagging the dog, Mike," warned Hope. "Do you listen when your customer tries to tell you how to install a toilet or frame a wall? Not a chance. That's because these are things you know how to do. You're in control, and you wouldn't dream of allowing a customer to start telling your crew how to build an addition. But you don't have the same level of confidence in your business practices, so you're more subject to being swayed. And you're afraid of losing customers. If you've explained how you operate right up front, before any contracts are signed, then there should be no questions. By the way, I've seen that customers who are kept in line will respect you more. Who's in charge of the project, Mike? You or the customer?"

## WHAT ABOUT TIME AND MATERIALS INVOICING?

"I guess I see your point," admitted Mike. "But what about if it's a time and materials job? I don't have a lot of them, but sometimes there's a situation where the whole project is one big set of unforeseen conditions, so I don't even really try to give a fixed price. If it's time and materials, how can I avoid giving them details about what each invoice is covering?"

"Ah, T&M is a different story," acknowledged Hope. "You're right, Mike, with T&M you do need to provide the customer with some information about the costs. However, I advise *against* doing what some companies do, which is to list everything on an invoice, give a subtotal, and then add another line item that contains the markup. I often see them label the additional item 'Overhead and profit.' There are three problems with this process. First, the more detail you give the customer, the more ammunition they have to complain. Second, if you do this, then you have to have a separate income account for the markup. That means that you won't have parallelism between your income and COGS accounts any more. Last, trust me, Mike, customers don't want to see the word 'profit' on an invoice!"

"But..." Mike protested....

"Listen, Mike, when you buy plywood, does the lumberyard show you the original cost and how much they mark it up? Your customers come to you because you're a professional. You have the experience and expertise they need. They have to pay for this. You need to stop feeling that you have to justify every penny of the customers' money and then justify your 'profit' on top of that."

"Yeah, but everyone invoices like that. So what do *you* think a T&M invoice should look like?" Mike still protested.

## PROVIDING T&M DETAIL

Hope took a deep breath, then smiled. "Well, you know the time we spent discussing the right amount of detail that you wanted to have for job costing? This is somewhat similar to that. You're going to need to decide exactly what you want to include in a T&M invoice, and then I'll help you create an invoice template and procedure to make that work for you. For example, maybe you just want to include some descriptive text that briefly tells what was done, and follow that with a single line item. Or maybe you want to have separate line items that subtotal labor, material, and subcontractor costs for that portion of work. Either way, it's important to include your markup within the price rather than having it sitting out there by itself."

Mike still seemed unconvinced. "Yeah, I guess I get your point, and I *do* like that parallelism thing that will let me see the margins for each type of income and cost. But I'm not sure I want to be a trendsetter. If everybody else is showing actual costs and then a markup figure that they've already discussed with the customer, I still may want to do it that way even if it means giving up the advantages of parallelism."

"You know, Mike," replied Hope after a moment's silence, "this is your company and all decisions must be yours. My job is to offer solutions and explain the consequences of your choices. If you really feel this is the way to go, then you'll need to add a new income account to your Chart of Accounts. You can call it 'Markup' or 'Contractor's fee' or something like that. Just be aware that if you're doing a mix of fixed price and T&M work, the numbers you get on your P&L won't be as easy to interpret. The contract price work will show the markup within the income categories, and the T&M work will show the markup in a separate account. This will make analysis challenging."

"Well, maybe I need to think more about this," said Mike slowly. "It *feels* different to me, but I guess if I present our way of doing things to the customer right from the start, there should be fewer problems. In the past, when customers asked me for stuff, I just reacted to shut them up since there was no policy. I guess I'll give it some thought."

## TRY DIFFERENT TEMPLATES TO GIVE YOU FLEXIBILITY

For the remainder of Hope's visit, she worked with Marci to demonstrate the various ways to generate an invoice from the estimate. Then Mike joined them and Hope showed several options for creating T&M invoices. By varying how costs were incorporated into the invoice, and by customizing invoice templates, Hope was able to produce several sample invoices with varying degrees of detail. Eventually, Mike chose a design and content that he felt comfortable with.

"We've accomplished a lot today," said Hope. "You've come a long way in terms of understanding your business, and it's been important for you to also learn a lot more about your accounting software. As the owner of the business, it's not your job to be the software expert, but it *is* your job to design an overall plan and to understand how your accounting software will be used to implement that plan. You also need to stick to the plan, remain consistent, and not ask your staff to do unnecessary work on a whim. I'm really pleased with what we've all achieved."

### What Mike learned:

1.  *On a fixed-price job, the payment schedule is an important part of the contract and should contain the right amount of detail to satisfy the customer without raising additional questions.*

2.  *On a fixed-price job, the purpose of the invoice (payment request) is to ask for money, not to report what was accomplished.*

3.  *On a T&M job, it may be risky to provide too much detail about individual purchases and line item costs.*

4.  *Regardless of how you invoice, it's critical to explain your system before the customer signs the contract.*

5.  *To keep analysis simple, treat income and costs for fixed-price and T&M jobs in a similar way.*

6. *It's my business and I can set the rules and policies, but I also must enforce them.*

## Self-assessment questions:

1. *Do you invoice according to policy or to meet the customer's demands?*

2. *Do you consider invoices to be payment requests or a tool for communicating job progress?*

3. *Have you ever provided additional information to a demanding customer who wanted more details than your system permits? And did it help or hurt?*

4. *When you go over your contract with a customer, how clearly and firmly do you present company policy regarding invoicing and payment schedule compliance?*

5. *If you create T&M invoices, do you include a line for "overhead and profit" on them?*

6. *Does the way that you invoice make P&L analysis simple?*

7. *On fixed-price jobs, are you invoicing from the estimate?*

8. *Do you sometimes feel like the customer is the one running your business?*

9. *Are you allowing customers' demands to add more work for your staff than originally planned, but not charging them for it?*

# Chapter 21 – A Little Extra Here and There, Please

When Hope arrived for the next appointment, she felt a certain degree of satisfaction at the "feel" of the office. Marci and Frankie were working quietly but industriously, and Mike was in his office actually looking at his financial reports. "Hey there!" said Mike heartily. "I bet you never expected to see me actually behaving like a numbers guy!"

## Using the Right Tools for Financial Management

"I'm impressed," laughed Hope. "Impressed, but not totally surprised. You've become aware that you *need* to understand financial concepts in order to run a company, but until recently you weren't really motivated to do so because you lacked the tools. There have been an awful lot of changes for you in the past few weeks. You should really be proud of what you and the team have accomplished in a short time."

"Well there is one thing that did occur to me after your last visit," Mike said. "We've talked about estimating a job, and then getting an estimate into my accounting system so we can use it as the basis for job costing, and also use it for creating invoices. Earlier you showed me how to calculate my overbillings and underbillings. I'm really getting that, and if every job went along without any changes, I can see how that would work just great. But in all the years that I've been in this business, I can't think of a single job where there weren't changes. That's the reality we live with. That formula you showed me before included a comparison of the actual costs to the estimated costs to figure out the percent complete. And you warned me that I have to make sure the estimated costs are accurate so I don't overstate the income. So can we talk about how to manage change orders and upgrades and extras and things like that?"

## CHANGE ORDERS WILL HAPPEN

Hope grinned. "I was wondering when you'd bring up change orders. Yes, in addition to my rule about all jobs starting after January 1 and ending before December 31, I'd like to suggest that once a contract is signed, *nobody* can ever change their mind. But we all know that's pie in the sky. And some contractors actually find that change orders can make them a lot of money."

Mike looked skeptical. "I know that we *believe* we have a process for handling change orders, but by the end of each job I always suspect that we've dropped the ball on things that should have been charged, or absorbed costs that really weren't part of the original contract. When you get a dozen or more change orders on a job, things can get really confusing. And customers don't seem to get that a change like making the toilet ivory instead of white is a lot different than deciding to add another dormer *after* the roof is already framed. It can be frustrating."

## SETTING EXPECTATIONS FOR CHANGE ORDERS

"I hear you," nodded Hope. "And we really need to look at several aspects of the change order process. First of all, you must make it very clear to the customer right from the start how change orders will be handled, and what the results will be. This should be spelled out in the contract, and you should also go over it verbally with all involved parties. So don't even think of explaining change orders to one person over the phone; wait until you have all the decision-making parties together face-to-face and explain the process carefully. I also suggest you review and confirm the policy at your pre-construction meetings."

"We do have a paragraph in our contract about change orders, but I think I need to go back and review it," admitted Mike. "Frankly, I just hoped that people read everything in the contract and I didn't take the time to read through it with them. I should probably make sure we go over something this important during my meeting with the customer."

156

## CHANGE ORDERS ADD MONEY <u>AND</u> TIME

"Exactly," agreed Hope. "One of the most important things for customers to understand about change orders is that not only will the *cost* (and therefore the overall price) of the job change, but often the *date* of completion will change. Mike, what kind of form are you currently using for change orders? Why don't you explain to me how a change order is processed, from the perspective of both the customer and of your company?"

Mike looked thoughtful. "As I said, I'd like to say that there is a process, but honestly I'd have to admit that change orders happen in lots of ways. Sometimes it's something simple at the job site, and the customer will just ask one of the guys to do something extra. The guy is supposed to tell Frankie, who is supposed to write it up. Then I *guess* Marci invoices for it, or maybe it gets added to the next scheduled payment. I'm not sure. Then other times the customer will call the office and talk with me or Frankie, and one of us will write up a change order and send it out for a signature. Sometimes I know that we go ahead and do whatever it is without a signature, especially if it's something simple and needs to be done right away to avoid holding up the job."

Mike paused, opened Excel, and located the change order form. "Here's what we use if we do actually send something out to the customer. Somebody created this for us years ago." (Refer Figure 21-1.)

| | |
|---|---|
| Customer Name | Date _____ |
| Change Order # | |
| Description of Change: | |
| | |
| Cost of Change Order | |
| Adjusted Contract Price | |
| | Approved by (for Company) — Date |
| | Agreed to (by Customer) — Date |

**Figure 21-1. Mike's current Change Order form.**

Hope spent some time looking at the form. "I see you have some good information here, Mike. You have a place for a description of the change, what it will cost the customer to make the change, the adjusted contract price – good job including that – and you require signatures from both the company and the customer. What I don't see here is the impact of the change order on the schedule, or the terms of payment. Maybe the terms are missing because you don't really have a policy about change order payments. Do you?"

Mike looked uncomfortable. "I think that like many other aspects of the business, in the past we've sort of done whatever seemed logical – or convenient, or comfortable – at the moment. What do you suggest?"

## WHEN SHOULD CHANGE ORDERS BE PAID FOR?

"Typically, I suggest that you get paid for change orders when they're signed. There are several reasons for this. First of all, it brings home to your customer the fact that changing their minds will, in most cases, cost them money. Making changes has consequences in terms of dollars, and often in terms of time. You don't necessarily want to discourage customers from making changes, especially if you're making a tidy margin on change orders, but they *must* feel the consequences. Also, even if you see change orders as a welcome addition to your profit, remember that changes that impact your schedule will mean a *lot* of work for your staff. It's the old domino effect. If the current job ends late, will your next job have to start late? If so, will your subs be able to accommodate the new schedule? And how much time will your staff have to spend informing subs and suppliers and re-scheduling deliveries or work? The impact of an altered schedule can be significant, and it's something that your customer can't be expected to understand. This is why I also suggest that you may want to put a higher markup on change order work to compensate for the additional effort and headaches that they often produce. Another consideration is that if you delay getting change orders paid for, you may risk having them build up, only to create a nasty surprise for your customer. I had a client who allowed $50,000 in change orders to accumulate throughout the job, and he hit the customer with them all at once at the end of the job. He was very, very lucky in that the customer paid them, but it left a bad taste right at the end of the job when you really want the customer to be happy with you."

"Oh, boy," Mike shook his head ruefully. "That brings back a bad memory. We had a similar situation where somehow the change orders just got away from us. The Farnsworths were a really nice older couple, and they were retired and hung around the job site a lot. They'd bring homemade cookies and lemonade and the crew just loved them. They kept finding lots of little things that they wanted the crew to do, and the crew would do them and then forget to tell the office. Anyway, all those little extras really added up once we sat down and figured it out. I was really shocked to see that it added up to over $10,000. Since I hated to hit them with that much, I just ate some of it. Even so, I know they just didn't understand why they ended up paying more than they planned."

"Uh-huh," Hope sympathized. "Sometimes, when you make a mistake, it's better to eat the dollars and salvage your reputation. But in general, I recommend that you avoid doing any work that's not included in the original contract *until* you have that signed change order. I know of many sad cases where additional work was performed without a written change order, and the customer refused to pay. In every instance I know of, when the contractor went to court, he lost. If you choose to perform extra work without a contract, you might as well wrap it with a bow because it'll be a gift to your customer."

"That makes sense," admitted Mike. "But what about the situation where my guys are in the middle of framing something and either the homeowners ask for a change that will mean the framing will have to be done differently, or we discover an error in the plans that need to be adjusted? There may not be time to stop, do an estimate, write up the change order, and get it signed. In that situation, isn't it better to just do the change and keep going so my guys aren't sitting around *waiting* for the paperwork?"

## WHAT ABOUT ON-THE-FLY CHANGES?

"I agree that's a tough one," admitted Hope, "and my suggestion would be to have some three-part carbonless forms made up just for this purpose and keep some right at the job site. If you progress to using a lead carpenter system, this is precisely the kind of thing that would be handled by your lead. He would write up a description of the change and price it if possible. If estimating the cost was impractical, he would put 'to be determined' in the blanks for cost and schedule adjustments, and at least get the darned thing signed. Then, he would keep one copy, give a copy to the customer, and send the third copy back to the office with his timecard. Now, at the very least, this indicates an agreement between the company and the customer that the work to be performed has been approved. You should also be *sure* that you get back to the customer within 24-48 hours. You can then provide a revised change order with the pricing and schedule information on it, accompanied by an invoice for any additional charges. However, since nobody in your existing crew has had sufficient training to perform this kind of task, I think it'll need to be up to Frankie to write up all the change orders for now. In the situation where the costs are unknown, Frankie will just have to put 'to be determined' for the cost and the time delay, but still get a signature from the customer. If Frankie can't get to the job site, you may – for the time being – provide some blank forms for the field crew. However, the rule must be that they will *not* be permitted to include any price quotes.

"Do you have somebody in the field that you think would be a good candidate for handling change orders, Mike? Maybe even somebody you could starting training to become a lead carpenter?"

"I'll have to give that some thought," said Mike. "But what you're suggesting in the meantime sounds workable. We've never gotten ourselves in serious trouble, mostly I think because our customers like us so much. But I've heard the horror stories too, and we can't just keep counting on good luck or nice customers. I agree we need to crack down on how we do things."

"So," said Hope, "let's look at creating a change order process. Then we need to modify your form to reflect that process. Finally, we'll need to review how change orders are addressed in your contract documentation.

"Your current form isn't bad, and we can just add some information that will make it better. I suggest we add more lines associated with the date of completion, and then make your payment policy clear right on this form."

## FORMS AND PROCESSES NEED TO WORK TOGETHER

After saving the company's original form in Excel, Hope made some adjustments to the form and then printed out a copy for Mike to review. (Refer Figure 21-2.)

Customer Name _____ Date _____

Change Order # _____

Description of Change: _____

_____

_____

_____

_____

_____

_____

_____

_____

Cost of Change Order _____

Adjusted Contract Price _____

Current estimated project completion date _____

Estimated effect on schedule as a result of this change order _____

Revised estimated project completion date _____

_____ _____
Approved by (for Company)                          Date

_____ _____
Agreed to (by Customer)                              Date

Payment for all change orders is due as of the date of the change order. A change order invoice will be issued upon signing. Work will not proceed on the change until the change order is signed and payment in full has been received.

**Figure 21-2. Mike's revised Change Order form.**

"OK," said Mike. "I do see that the additional information makes things clearer. Can we just start using this right away?"

"Absolutely, but remember that a form without a process isn't very effective," cautioned Hope. "We need to talk about the mechanics of how change orders happen, who will be authorized to create and price them, and what the paperwork trail will be. Don't forget that if the change order agreement is going to be followed by a change order invoice, Marci will need to be in the loop. Let's talk about how this will work."

After some discussion, Hope and Mike decided that all requested changes would be directed to Frankie until a lead carpenter system could be implemented. New company policy would ask customers to contact Frankie directly rather than discussing changes with field workers. In a situation in which the change would directly impact work in progress, a designated crewmember would be authorized to complete a proposed change order form, get signatures, and then notify Frankie immediately. The worker creating the change order would also note it on his daily timecard as well as attaching a copy of the proposed change order to the timecard. Marci would then get a heads up about the change from the paperwork and make sure to communicate with Frankie so she could invoice it as soon as possible.

"This sounds like a good plan for the time being," said Hope. "And as you move toward a lead carpenter system, you can review and revise this process."

## UPDATE YOUR FINANCIAL INFORMATION WITH CHANGE ORDERS

"Another thing we need to consider," Hope said, "is how all of this is handled in your accounting software. Remember that the costs shown in your job cost reports are comparing the original estimated costs. It's important to note that you will need to keep the estimated costs *including change orders* up to date in order to avoid looking like you're over budget or more complete than you are."

"Yeah, that makes sense. But it doesn't seem that important," Mike protested.

"Let's say that your original estimate showed a cost of $500 for a shower unit. That means in a job cost report, the estimated cost would show $500. But if the customer decides to upgrade to a spa unit with a cost of $3,500, unless you get the additional estimated cost included in the report, when you buy that spa unit for $3,500, the job cost report will still show an estimated cost of $500 while the actual cost is $3,500. You will appear to be over budget by $3,000.

"Also, if you are calculating the percentage of completion for the whole job, it will look like you're further along than you really are. Does that make sense?"

"Oh," nodded Mike. "So I can see that if we're trying to compare estimated costs to actual costs, then we need to make sure we're including *all* the estimated costs, *including* those costs related to accepted change orders. I get it."

162

"Now I'm going to show Marci how to make this happen in QuickBooks," concluded Hope. "Mike, your homework for next time is to review how change orders are spelled out in your current contract and revise it to reflect the process we've just created. Make sure you have your lawyer review and approve any changes to the contract as well."

### *What Mike learned:*

1. *Change orders can be profitable, but only if they're handled reliably and consistently, using a well-defined process, and the customer actually pays for them.*

2. *Forms should be designed to implement and reinforce policy and should be kept as simple as possible.*

3. *Important policies such as the handling of change orders should not be left for the customer to read about on their own; they need to be explained in advance of buying the job.*

4. *Change orders are potentially disruptive and need to be sold with enough margin to cover the inconvenience; this should be explained to customers from the start.*

5. *Change orders should be dealt with and paid for immediately and not allowed to accumulate.*

6. *Change orders can impact the job's scheduled completion date, and customers as well as the production team need to be kept informed of any modifications to the original completion date.*

7. *Change orders affect estimated costs as well as revenue, and financial software must reflect all changes.*

### *Self-assessment questions:*

1. *How much money do you think you've lost on unbilled change order work?*

2. *Are you making money on your change order work?*

3. *Is your crew working for you or the customer?*

4. *How well does your change order process work for you?*

5. *What's the time frame from change order discussion to payment for the change order?*

6. *Are change orders sometimes caused by inadequate discussion with customers before you completed their proposals?*

# CHAPTER 22 – DON'T GET BURIED WITH PAPERWORK

As soon as Hope arrived, Mike was anxious to show off the changes he had made to the contract, including the change order process. He had even sent it to his lawyer to get her blessing. He also reported that the revised change order form had already been ordered and should be ready by the end of the week. Finally, Mike had called a brief meeting the day before Hope arrived to explain the new change order process to both office and production staff.

"That sounds like real progress," Hope congratulated Mike. "How did the meeting go?"

## TEAM BUY-IN ON NEW PROCEDURES

"Well, it was a little different this time," said Mike with a hint of a smile. "In the past, when we've tried to implement a new idea, I've run into everything from obvious, loud complaints to stone cold silence. This time I came to the meeting having already made the decisions and with some printed samples of the new form. I had a really clear vision of *why* we were making a change and starting a new procedure; I included the reasons for this change when I explained the process. I even passed out copies of the new form to everyone. Nobody said anything negative, I didn't see the usual eyeball rolling, and the meeting lasted all of fifteen minutes. I think it went really well."

"I'm glad to hear it," noted Hope, "but I'm not surprised. Once you have a clear idea of what you're trying to accomplish (or what you're trying to avoid!), and you've thought through the process and prepared any associated support materials, you'll be more likely to speak with conviction. Too often, owners go to a show or read an article and then come back with some great idea that they then try to foist on their employees without putting effort into seeing whether or not it's a great idea *for this company*. You can't just stick something new into a company without taking the time to think about how existing processes may need to be modified. For example, do you think it would have made a difference if you'd gone into the meeting, announced that now some of the production workers may have to write up proposed change orders, and then had no form to show them?"

"Yeah," admitted Mike. "I don't think they would have taken me seriously. And the meeting would probably have turned into a two-hour marathon discussion of the pros and cons. In thinking back now to some of my less-well-received announcements, I can see that I wasn't really that sure *myself* how the new thing would work; just that it felt like a good idea and assumed that everybody would sort of figure it out on their own."

"Uh-huh. And how did that work for you?" Hope teased. "We've spent a lot of time together analyzing how you do things, we've put together some practical strategies for avoiding past problems, and your office staff is now working like a team. This gives you more time to actually manage your company. And as you know, the highest value you will probably get from your financial software is its use as a management tool. And that means we need to start looking at reports."

## REPORTS HAVE DIFFERENT LEVELS OF DETAIL

Hope went on to open up the accounting software in Mike's office and walk him through the various reports. "I think of reports in terms of what I like to call forest, grove, and trees," she explained. "Imagine flying a small plane over a forest. The view as you pass over would be pretty general. You would get a good sense of the size and shape of the forest, and maybe you could tell there were small clearings in it or that there were more conifers than deciduous trees, but overall you'd be seeing very little detail. Your basic financial reports such as your P&L and Balance Sheet are 'forest-level' reports: they tell you about how your company is doing overall. Remember when we talked about *not* using your P&L for job costing? The reason is that at the 'forest-level' view, you don't want to be trying to identify which species of trees are in the forest. You just want to understand its overall size and shape. At the other end of the spectrum are the 'tree-level' reports. These might include job cost detail reports for a single job, or a listing of all purchases from a particular vendor. In between, you'll find the 'grove-level' reports. These will be more specific than the 'forest-level' reports, and less detailed than the 'tree-level' reports. Examples might include reports like the P&L by Job, Sales by Customer, or the Accounts Payable Aging report. Does this make sense?"

"Yeah, it does," Mike nodded. "I know that I've been really confused about all the reports that are available. I never knew what was in each one, or which ones mattered most. Half the time I couldn't find a report that I'd stumbled onto in the past, and that was really frustrating. Or Marci would bring me a stack of paper that should have made sense but didn't. And to top it off, I didn't really trust the information that I was looking at anyway. Thinking about all the reports this way makes it simpler. And I bet you're going to tell me that some people need to be looking at forest reports while others stick with tree reports, right?"

## DIFFERENT PEOPLE NEED DIFFERENT REPORTS

Hope laughed. "You nailed that one, Mike. For example, is it useful or even appropriate for Frankie to be monitoring your P&L? No. However, it's going to be *part of his job* to monitor the tree-level job cost reports. Who *does* need to be looking at the P&L, Mike?" Hope asked with a twinkle in her eye.

"Well, I'm thinking that would be *me*," Mike grinned back.

"Correct, you are!" said Hope. "While different software can call different reports by different names, they usually have pretty similar reports. Since you have QuickBooks, let's look at the reports you can get out of your software."

## EXPLORE ALL AVAILABLE REPORTS

Hope walked Mike through the different QuickBooks reporting menus, and Mike was quickly able to figure out for himself whether any given report was at the forest, grove, or tree level. Hope tracked some of the results in a spreadsheet. (Refer Figure 22-1.)

| Name of report | Forest | Grove | Tree |
|---|---|---|---|
| P&L Standard (& with prev year) | X | | |
| Balance Sheet Standard | X | | |
| Job Profitability Summary | X | | |
| P&L by Job | | X | |
| P&L Detail | | | X |
| Job Costs by Vendor & Job Summary | | X | |
| Job Costs by Job & Vendor Summary | | X | |
| Expenses by Vendor Summary | | X | |
| Expenses by Vendor Detail | | | X |
| Accounts Receivable Aging Summary | | X | |
| Open Invoices | | | X |
| Transaction List by Customer | | | X |
| Transaction List by Account | | | X |
| Sales by Customer Summary | | X | |
| Job Estimates vs. Actuals Summary | | X | |
| Job Estimates vs. Actuals Detail | | | X |
| Time by Job Detail | | | X |
| Accounts Payable Aging Summary | | X | |
| Unpaid Bills Detail | | | X |
| Payroll Summary | | X | |
| Unpaid Bills by Job | | | X |
| Open Purchase Orders by Job | | | X |

**Figure 22-1. Forest, grove, and tree reports in QuickBooks.**

"The next step," Hope noted, "will be to determine which reports should be run or reviewed by which people. And how often. In your case, you may want to receive printed copies of specific reports on a regular basis: for example, maybe you want to see a Job Profitability Summary report on a weekly basis and a P&L Standard on a monthly basis, once Marci has made the WIP adjustments. Depending on how frequently you pay your bills, you may want to see your Accounts Payable Aging Summary every week so you can approve which bills are to be paid. You will be concerned with the forest and grove reports.

"Typically, others in your company will be reviewing tree-level reports. Unless it's a very small company, the owner typically delegates to others the task of monitoring highly detailed reports. The frequency with which reports are reviewed depends on several parameters. First, let's think about financial reports. If you're entering WIP adjustments on a monthly basis, there's no real point in checking your P&L more frequently than at the end of each month."

"OK, I get that," nodded Mike. "Since the WIP adjustment is supposed to give me a more accurate gross margin, looking at the P&L before it's adjusted won't really tell me much. In fact, that's sort of what I had before: lots of ups and downs that just confused me."

## LOOK AT JOB COST REPORTS

"Exactly right," agreed Hope. "Now let's consider job reports. First of all, you'll probably be depending on Frankie to monitor these, since he's your production manager. How often Frankie reviews reports on individual jobs will depend on how long each job lasts. For example, if your jobs typically last only two or three days, then there's no point in looking at a whole bunch of individual jobs every day. Instead, he'd want to look at a grove-level report on a weekly or twice-monthly basis. The grove-level report would be set up to show trends for several similar jobs: by type of job, by sales price, or by some other criteria."

"But most of our jobs last for several months," said Mike. "So how often should Frankie be checking them out? I assume he's going to want to monitor things pretty carefully throughout the whole job, right?"

## JOB COST REPORTS CAN HELP YOU FIND SLIPPAGE

"Absolutely," agreed Hope. "Looking at individual job cost reports can be extremely important. You want to be sure that things are progressing on budget, that no change order costs show up without matching revenue, and that you don't see odd costs show up that weren't included in the estimate. But one of the basic reasons to review job cost reports is to look for slippage. Remember, slippage is an industry term for a reduced gross margin caused by cost overruns. It's critical to track slippage in order to correct your estimating system. You should pay particular attention to areas of slippage that are consistent among jobs. For example, I had a client who was always over his estimated costs on trim because his personal standards were very high. Once the crew had finished, this guy would go check on the job, and if there was something that wasn't perfect, he'd have the crew re-do it. This kind of behavior was putting him over his trim budget on nearly all his jobs, yet he continued to estimate trim in the same old way. He should have either stopped being so picky, or he should have started estimating a higher figure for trim work. Since he never got around to altering the way he estimated *or* changing his behavior, he was never able to eliminate the slippage and the benefit of doing the job costing was lost. So I recommend that when you review job cost reports, you focus on areas of slippage that are common to multiple jobs. This is a sure sign of the need to revise your estimating assumptions. And most important, when you do find some consistent estimating errors, *apply what you learn to the way you estimate*."

Given that it now looked like Mike wasn't expected to run, analyze, and act on every single report, he was looking relieved. "So can we go over who should be running which reports, and how often? I think it would be good to come up with a checklist so everybody will know what's expected."

## DETERMINE THE "WHO" AND "WHEN" OF REPORTS

"Great idea," agreed Hope.

Together they produced a master list of reports and assigned responsibility and frequency to each report. (Refer Figure 22-2.) They also discussed how the resulting reports should be used. For example, once Marci ran a weekly Accounts Payable Summary along with a report showing vendor discount cutoff dates, she would give the report to Mike for approval prior to creating payments.

| Name of report | Who | When |
|---|---|---|
| P&L Standard (& with prev year) | Mike | Monthly |
| Balance Sheet Standard | Mike | Monthly |
| Job Profitability Summary | Mike | Monthly |
| P&L by Job | Mike | Monthly |
| P&L Detail | Marci | Monthly |
| Job Costs by Vendor & Job Summary | Frankie | Monthly |
| Job Costs by Job & Vendor Summary | Frankie | Monthly |
| Expenses by Vendor Summary | Marci | On demand |
| Expenses by Vendor Detail | Marci | On demand |
| Accounts Receivable Aging Summary | Marci | Weekly |
| Open Invoices | Marci | Weekly |
| Transaction List by Customer | Marci | On demand |
| Transaction List by Account | Marci | On demand |
| Sales by Customer Summary | Marci | Monthly |
| Job Estimates vs. Actuals Summary | Mike | Monthly |
| Job Estimates vs. Actuals Detail | Frankie | Weekly |
| Time by Job Detail | Frankie | On demand |
| Accounts Payable Aging Summary | Marci | Weekly |
| Unpaid Bills Detail | Marci | On demand |
| Payroll Summary | Marci | Each Pay Period |
| Unpaid Bills by Job | Frankie | On demand |
| Open Purchase Orders by Job | Frankie | Weekly |

**Figure 22-2. Master list of reports with responsibility and frequency .**

"You know," remarked Mike, as he scanned the list of reports, "this isn't that bad. I can see that as the owner, it's my job to review just the forest-type reports. Sure, I want to have control over which bills we pay, but as long as there's a system for giving me a report each week, all I really need to do is look for anything out of the ordinary. And if we can count on more regular cash flow, I won't have the headache of trying to figure out what percentage of whose bill I tell Marci to pay. I can be proactive instead of reactive!"

# CUTTING MIKE LOOSE

"I couldn't have said it better myself, Mike!" smiled Hope. "In fact, that brings me to another point. You have come really far since our first meeting. Think about how much you've accomplished! I'm thrilled that you've absorbed so much and have already implemented many improved practices. There is more *purpose* now in your company's daily operations. You're starting to get *meaningful* information from reports that are not only accurate, but now *make sense to you*. I'm so confident that you really have a better understanding of your business that I don't need to come back for while. How about we schedule my next visit in around six to eight weeks so I can check on your progress? Let's see how your systems are working, whether the job coding is going well, and what you're learning from your reports. We can tweak anything that needs it, and I'm going to ask you, Frankie, and Marci to each keep a list of questions. But until then, Mike, I'm cutting you loose. Congratulations!"

Mike looked both pleased and slightly apprehensive as he shook Hope's hand. "It's taken us a while to get to this point," he commented, "but I think we're ready to do this! Thanks for bringing us this far, and I'm really looking forward to seeing how things run. I have no illusions about the likelihood of a few bumps, but I'm feeling pretty confident overall. Let's set a date."

### *What Mike learned:*

1. *Although there are literally hundreds of reports available, not all reports have to be used at all, all the time, or by everybody.*

2. *The job of the owner is to review reports produced by others on a regular basis.*

3. *There is no point in running reports more often than they are updated or adjusted.*

4. *Owners are more likely to use "forest-level" and "grove-level" reports for management purposes.*

5. *Owners should be looking for trends.*

6. *Project managers need to stay on top of active jobs via job cost reports.*

7. *Project managers should watch for slippage – and watch even more closely for common areas of slippage among different jobs so the information can be used to improve future estimates.*

### Self-Assessment Questions:

1. Do you have a checklist of reports that should be generated regularly?

2. Do you regularly review a set group of reports?

3. Are you actually looking at the reports that others produce for you and do they make sense?

4. Do you feel you are looking at the right reports?

5. Do you act on the information gleaned from the reports you review?

6. Are you confident that the reports you look at are correct and current? Do you regularly make corrections so the reports continue to be accurate and meaningful?

7. Do you compare current reports with similar ones from past periods to see trends?

8. Do you get too involved with the detail and miss the forest for the trees?

9. Are your Chart of Accounts and job cost categories set up to give you the right level of reporting?

# Epilogue – Six Months Later

It was late on a Friday afternoon. Marci had just brought Mike the month-end reports as usual when Frankie appeared at the door to Mike's office. He too was clutching a small pile of reports, and he grinned when he saw Marci in the office, leaning over Mike's desk and pointing to a particular line item on one of the reports.

"Ha! Beat me to it, eh?" he joked. When Marci looked somewhat confused, he explained. "I just meant that I'm here to deliver *my* reports to Mike as well, but I see you're in line ahead of me. This sort of thing wouldn't have happened in the old days – neither of us would have done this."

"You mean the bad old days," corrected Mike. "Yeah, I guess things have changed around here since Hope stirred things up. I hadn't really thought about it recently."

## Change for the Better

There was a small pause as all three silently reviewed what the changes had meant to them personally, as well as to the company. Frankie casually laid his reports on the corner of Mike's desk and sat down. "Hey, Mike, what's been the biggest difference for you over the past six months?" asked Frankie.

Mike pondered the question for a few moments as Marci quietly took a seat next to Frankie. "I guess the biggest change is the amount of time I'm spending at the office. Production is running better, and there aren't as many problems, so I don't feel like I have to drive out to the job site every hour to pick up the pieces after the latest disaster. I've been able to hang up my Superman cape even though I'm still tempted to be a hero. Of course," Mike continued with a twinkle, "the nice thing about having to jump back into production was that it was a really *great* excuse for not coming in *here*. I always felt like the minute I appeared, you guys would pounce on me with a million questions. I hated that. Now that there's a system for handling the routine stuff, you two ask me questions – what, maybe three or four times a week?"

## HIDING FROM PROBLEMS NEVER WORKS

"Yeah, about that," Marci chimed in. "And you used to sort of duck into your office like I couldn't *see* you or something. Actually, it was pretty funny in retrospect, but it used to annoy the heck out of me back then." She paused, then observed, "Lots of things used to annoy me then because I hated not being able to check things off my list. It always seemed like I couldn't get out payroll because somebody didn't bother to get his timecard in on time, or I couldn't get out an invoice because somebody *thought* there might be a change order, or I couldn't pay a bill because Mike wasn't around to give the thumbs up, or something like that. It was awful. And frustrating."

"But you hid it well," observed Frankie with a note of sarcasm. All three laughed and Frankie admitted, "You weren't exactly my favorite person back then, which I find hard to believe now that we're working so closely together on a daily basis. I can't even remember the last time I wanted to wring your neck!"

"Or I yours!" Marci retorted. "But having these new systems when things are going smoothly is one thing. We've run into some situations where – thank heaven – we not only had a system but people actually stuck to it. Do you remember Mrs. Brooks?"

## USING SYSTEMS TO STAY OUT OF TROUBLE

"Yeah, that was a great example of dodging a bullet just by doing things by the book," acknowledged Mike. "She was *such* a nice little old lady that I am 100% sure that without the new change order procedure, the production guys would have done what they did with the Farnsworths in the past: kept doing 'little things' for them, not writing it up because they *always* seemed to be such little things, and then eventually letting the office know about what should have been about thirty change orders. And back then, we ate a bunch of it, of course, to save our reputation. This time, though, everybody did what they were supposed to do. The change orders got written up, there were no surprises, and Mrs. Brooks became one of our raving fans even though she spent nearly $23,000 in change orders. That was a lot of money to her, but she thought carefully about every change and made an informed decision knowing at the time exactly what it would add to her price and completion date."

"Speaking of jobs that are going smoothly," Frankie interjected, "hadn't you just sold the Wiley job when Hope first came? I don't even think we'd started it yet."

"Hey, you're right," Mike agreed. "In fact, even though I was really upset when I figured out that I'd sold it too cheaply, we've done pretty well on it. Things have gone fairly smoothly, and we've upped our achieved margin a bit by pricing the change orders properly. And I seem to recall that a few of them have been ones that you caught, Frankie."

## REPORTS CAN SAVE YOU MONEY AND MAKE YOU MORE PROFITABLE

"Yup. Now that we're getting reports that show labor by dollars *and* time, I was able to spot those couple of overruns that didn't look right...."

"...and once you brought them to my attention," Mike continued, "I went back over the scope of work with the Wileys and we agreed that the overruns were due to some extras that sort of slipped in there. With better communication and advance warning, they paid for the resulting change orders without question. That's exactly the sort of thing that we wouldn't have noticed in the past. Or if we did figure it out, it would have been at the end of the job when it was too late to mention. So we'd just end up eating it."

"And speaking of overruns," Frankie recalled, "now that we're managing costs better through PO's, Marci's been able to save us some bucks. Remember that lumberyard bill that didn't even belong to us?"

## USING PURCHASE ORDERS CAN SAVE YOU MONEY

Marci grinned. "Oh, yeah. They accidentally charged another company's delivery to our account. It was pretty obvious since there wasn't a matching PO, and I was able to get it straightened out quickly. I'm pretty sure that in the past I would have spotted it sooner or later, but it would have taken quite a while to track it down. We used to have so many people placing orders back then, and nothing was coded, so I would have wasted a lot of time chasing everybody to get more information. It may even have taken so much time that we would have paid the bill by the 10th of the month to get our discount, and then had to wait months for the credit. That sort of thing really messed with our cash flow. The PO system really helped again when one of the electrical subs accidentally double-charged us."

"Or maybe it wasn't an accident," commented Frankie. "We'll never know, but either way, you sure caught it fast."

"One case that *wasn't* so obvious was that drywall guy. What was his name?" Frankie asked.

"Dave. Dave's Drywall," Mike recalled with annoyance. "Not only did he want 100% of his fee up front, but he wouldn't send us his workers' comp certificate. He showed up here one day looking for work and our regular drywall company was unavailable for a small upcoming job, so I thought I'd take a chance. I almost caved, but Marci held my feet to the fire and insisted we follow procedure. No insurance certificate, no work."

"Good thing you listened, Mike," laughed Frankie. "Didn't we hear a month later that the guy had taken some other contractor for a *lot* of money, and then disappeared? Another bullet dodged!"

Marcie added, "What would you have done a year ago when we got that really big health insurance hike recently? I bet you would have just paid it. But Hope suggested we keep the company contribution to a dollar figure instead, which we did. When the increase hit, our costs stayed the same. That saved us some bucks! Even though the guys grumbled a bit, they all admitted that they didn't realize how much the insurance cost. Mike, it was great that you didn't cave in to their whining."

## STICKING TO YOUR GUNS

"I realize that I'm always going to have to fight my tendency to cave in," admitted Mike, "especially when people whine. I know in the past, I've always backed down when a customer whined about price because I like being the 'good guy.' However, now that I *know* my numbers, and *believe* that the price I quote is what I *should* charge, it's a lot easier to stick to my guns. I used to leave a lot of money on the table. Of course, now that you guys are here to keep me on the straight and narrow, it's easier to argue with subs, suppliers, and customers than it is to argue with my own team! You sure were right about Chris."

"Well, it took some effort to convince you," recalled Frankie, "but by reviewing timecards, both Marci and I had noticed that he was not as productive as everyone else. He just wasn't showing the same proportion of billable time as other guys. We'd all heard the grumbling about him before; several of the crew had badmouthed him to me, and I'd passed the word to you. But without good data, I think it was easier for us to just pass it off as a personality conflict or something. Marci was really the one who pushed the issue; she doesn't have any real ties with the crew, so I think it's a little easier for her to be objective."

"Yeah, dealing with the crew always drove me nuts and I know they felt the same way about me," agreed Marci. "I'd always have to chase them down for information, or missing timecards, or whatever. Now it's pretty rare for me to chase *anybody*. And didn't you get some good feedback after you finally got rid of Chris, Mike?"

## PRODUCTIVITY CAN BE MEASURED

"That was the real surprise," admitted Mike. "I was dreading the whole experience, but once I was certain the guy wasn't pulling his weight and we set up specific, measurable goals for him, it was clear he couldn't cut it. And Chris realized that too. So, when he left, the rest of the crew was delighted. I was afraid they'd blame me for his leaving, but they told me they felt it was unfair that Chris was getting paid the same as everyone else for doing less work, and they actually thanked me for getting rid of him. It ended up actually *helping* morale. I didn't see that coming. Hey, maybe that's the key to success: just keep firing people!"

"Hey, watch it!" laughed Marci. "I've already cut back my hours to 30 a week."

## KEEP VALUABLE EMPLOYEES BY BEING FLEXIBLE

"Speaking of that, how are your classes going, Marci?" asked Mike. "When you first told me you wanted to go back to school to get your accounting degree I was afraid we were going to lose you. I know you've been able to keep on top of things here in the office because everything's always done on time. How about school?"

"It's really worked out well. I'm taking only two courses at a time, and they're both in the morning. So I can work around them and still get things done here. Now that we've started implementing the lead carpenter system, the leads are doing a much better job ordering the right materials and pre-coding the purchase orders. That, and the better cash flow that allows us to pay most bills as they're due, has made my job much easier. I'm less stressed out about work, I love my classes and my job, and now I can do both. By the way, Mike, I do appreciate your flexibility given that my class times change each semester. I can always get in all my hours, but they do tend to vary from week to week."

"Hey, I'm just glad you're willing to keep working here, and I'm impressed at how much you're able to accomplish, even with reduced hours. In fact, now that I'm spending more time in the office, it's easier for me to see what's going on here. I already admitted that I hated coming in here before, and because I was rarely here, it was hard to understand – and appreciate – what was going on. I'm more confident about things being under control, both in the field and here." Mike added, "And I think focusing on the timecards has really improved field-office communications. The guys finally get how important it is for us to know what they're doing and how long it takes. By now they've stopped thinking that we were somehow trying to spy on them or something when we asked them to categorize their work."

Frankie added, "Another benefit of having the production guys recording time by specific categories is that I've been able to see how much time they're spending doing setup, cleanup, organizing materials, and so forth. That stuff has to be done but isn't really what you think of when you think of production. Every time I'm at the job site and see our best carpenter pushing a broom or unloading a truck, I cringe. Now that we all agree on the categories, I'm getting better information and can plan and manage the jobs better."

## THINK OUTSIDE THE BOX

"One of your best suggestions, Frankie," noted Mike approvingly, "was to hire Pete to free up the more experienced (and more expensive) guys from the grunt work. He's part time so we don't have to offer him benefits. It's been great that he's been able to work here while he's taking classes at the local vocational technical school. He's a bright, motivated young guy who's been perfectly happy to learn the trade from the ground up while he makes a little money. It's a win-win solution, and it's meant that we haven't had to replace Chris. Again, thanks to you, Frankie, we've cut our production labor costs."

Frankie jumped in, "And that lead carpenter thing is really starting to pay off. Now that Al is in training to be a lead carpenter, I can finally start acting like a true production manager. I can oversee jobs instead of getting buried in all the time-consuming detail work like ordering and chasing subs."

"Yeah," noted Mike, "it's great that instead of just wasting your time running from job to job, you're actually overseeing, analyzing, and keeping the jobs on track. And I know that you're providing Al with a lot of training and support."

## GROWING WITH A LEAD CARPENTER SYSTEM

"Yup," said Frankie. "Al has worked out great. Let's keep on the lookout for more good talent. If we keep growing like we've done in the last six months, we're going to need more lead carpenters. I've notice that the job runs smoother when we have both a lead carpenter and laborer, like Al and Pete, on the job. And Al has really stepped up to the plate to take on more day-to-day responsibility for managing the job. I've also noticed that some of the other guys are taking more interest in the management side of things. Maybe one of them will have what it takes to become our next lead carpenter."

Marci added, "Yeah, and now that you have time to keep on top of the costs, this lead carpenter system is really helping the bottom line."

"Absolutely," agreed Mike. "And Frankie's been watching those job cost reports like a hawk. Hope suggested that we not only monitor the reports, but look for similar overrun categories among jobs. Remember that story she told about a client of hers who consistently underestimated trim? Well, Frankie discovered that Hope actually had *two clients* who underestimate trim – and I was the other one! Frankie had to sort of rub my nose in it, but now I really believe that I need to estimate based on my *crew*'s productivity, not some memory of how fast *I could have done it* when I was in the field. Of course, without reports that *both* make sense to me *and* I can trust, it would have been a hard sell to make me change. The jobs that I've estimated since then have been much more realistic, and we're coming much closer to hitting our labor budget. I really feel like I'm getting a handle on slippage. While I know we can't get rid of it altogether, we are certainly controlling it better than before. What a change!"

Marci and Frankie nodded simultaneously and exchanged knowing looks with a grin. "You can say *that* again!" said Frankie. "It seems to me that we were all operating in the dark before. Marci rarely received complete information about *anything*. And frankly it seemed like Mike spent most of his time running around putting out fires, hiding from the office, and duplicating everything I did as a production manager. Hey, Mike, since you're no longer doing *my job* as well as your own, you must have a little more time now."

## TRUSTING THE TEAM

At this, Mike smiled broadly. "Well, not only have I been actually taking weekends off, but now my wife sees me at least as much as my customers do," he chuckled. "That's a big improvement!

"To tell you the truth," he continued more seriously, "my son will be old enough to start Little League next year, and I'm thinking about being a coach. Now I can trust my company team and the systems we've implemented. You guys have been great! I can monitor the company's progress through those reports you guys give me instead of running around trying to micromanage everything. That whole work-life balance that I thought was pie in the sky sure makes sense now. When my buddy George talked with me about getting his life back, I frankly didn't believe him. Now I get what he was talking about when he suggested I hire Hope. While it's been a struggle at times, I can see that together, you guys have helped me build a better company and we're on the right track."

# Appendix A – Glossary of Financial and Accounting Terms

**Above the line** ABOVE THE LINE in construction business accounting generally refers to job-related or direct costs. "The Line" is the line that subtotals all job-related (or Cost of Goods Sold) costs on the Profit and Loss Statement. Any costs above this line are subtracted to obtain the Gross Margin. Any costs below that line would be included in Overhead. Since job-related costs appear *above* this line, they are said to be "above the line." See also Cost of Goods Sold.

**Accounts Payable** ACCOUNTS PAYABLE (A/P) is the total of all trade accounts representing obligations to pay for goods and services received. In most accounting systems, Accounts Payable is considered a "control account" where the total balance is further broken down by individual vendors.

**Accounts Receivable** ACCOUNTS RECEIVABLE (A/R) is a current asset representing money due from customers for services performed or merchandise sold on credit. In most accounting systems, Accounts Receivable is considered a "control account" where the total balance is further broken down by individual customers.

**Accrual basis** ACCRUAL BASIS is an accounting method whereby income is recognized (appears on the Profit and Loss Statement) at the time it is earned or invoiced. Expenses appear when they are incurred. Because the Profit and Loss Statement shows income and costs as they occur, rather than when they are received or paid, it is a better way to manage profitability. See Cash Basis for alternative accounting method.

**Accumulated Depreciation** ACCUMULATED DEPRECIATION is the cumulative amount of depreciation that has been expensed on the Profit and Los Statement over the life of the asset. For example, if you purchase a used truck for $20,000 and depreciate it $4,000 per year over five years, the amount in the accumulated depreciate account at the end of three years will be $12,000.

**Assets**          ASSETS represent what a business owns or is due. Cash, Accounts Receivable, prepaid expenses, vehicles and equipment are all examples of assets. Typical categories include Current assets, Fixed assets, and Other assets. Current assets refers to cash, Account Receivable or any asset that is or will be converted to cash within the next twelve months. Fixed assets refers to vehicles and equipment or any asset that provides value over more than one accounting period. Other assets include any assets which do not easily fit into the previous categories.

**Audit Trail**     AUDIT TRAIL is a step-by-step record by which all transactions are traced. In QuickBooks, the Audit Trail is always on and tracks all changes made to transactions, including the date and time of change, and the user making the change.

**Balance Sheet**   BALANCE SHEET is a standard accounting report that provides a "snapshot" view of all assets, liabilities, and equity (including net profit) as of a given point in time. You need to review both the Balance Sheet and the Profit and Loss Statement to verify accuracy since most errors on the Balance Sheet mean that the Profit and Loss Statement is also inaccurate.

The Balance Sheet formula is Assets = Liabilities + Equity.

**Bank Reconciliation**   BANK RECONCILIATION is the verification of a bank statement balance and the company's checkbook balance.

**Below the line**  BELOW THE LINE in construction business accounting generally refers to overhead or indirect costs. "The Line" is the line that subtotals all job-related (or Cost of Goods Sold) costs on the Profit and Loss Statement. Any costs above this line are subtracted to obtain the Gross Margin. Any costs below that line would be included in overhead. Costs related to maintaining the company appear below this line in a Profit and Loss and are therefore said to be "below the line." See also Above the line, Overhead, G&A.

**Bill**            BILL is a term typically used to describe a purchase invoice (example: an invoice from a vendor or subcontractor). In QuickBooks, invoices refer specifically to sales invoices while purchase invoices are called bills.

**Billable Hours**  BILLABLE HOURS refers to hours worked on a job. These hours should be job costed and can be included in invoices to customers.

**Billings in Excess of Costs**  BILLINGS IN EXCESS OF COSTS see OVERBILLINGS.

**Break-Even Analysis**  BREAK-EVEN ANALYSIS is an analysis method used to determine the total dollar volume of sales required to reach a projected gross profit amount or an amount equal to overhead.

**Budget-Job**  See Estimate

**Burden Rate**  BURDEN RATE is the sum of employer costs over and above salaries (including employer taxes, benefits, etc.). It is usually calculated on production personnel in order to understand the entire cost to put an employee in the field.

**Cash Basis**  CASH BASIS is an accounting method whereby income is recognized (appears on the Profit and Loss Statement) at the time the money is received. Expenses appear once they are paid. Because the Profit and Loss Statement shows income and costs as they are paid or received, rather than when they occur, it is less useful as a management tool. However, it may be advantageous to file your tax return on a cash basis depending on IRS regulations. See Accrual Basis for alternative accounting method.

**Chart of Accounts**  CHART OF ACCOUNTS is a list of ledger account names and associated numbers arranged in the order in which they normally appear in the financial statements. The Chart of Accounts is customarily arranged in the following order: Assets, Liabilities, Owners' Equity (Stockholders' Equity for a corporation), Revenue, Cost of Goods Sold (COGS) and Expenses.

**COGS**  See Cost of Goods Sold

**Consumables**  CONSUMABLES are items purchased and used on jobs but are small in nature and often purchased in bulk. It may not be practical to attribute them to individual jobs, but may be allocated to jobs on some other basis. Examples include sanding disks, Sawzall blades, and contractor bags.

**Cost in Excess of Billings**  See Underbillings

**Contract Price**  CONTRACT PRICE refers to the act of selling a job for a fixed amount. It is also called Fixed Price.

| | |
|---|---|
| **Cost of Goods Sold (COGS)** | COST OF GOODS SOLD (COGS) is a group of accounts on the Profit and Loss Statement associated with the production of a specific job. Included are materials, subcontractors, production labor costs, and equipment rented specifically for a job. See Above the line, Job-related costs. |
| **Cost Code** | COST CODE is used to provide the job cost breakdown outside of the Profit and Loss Statement. Examples of common cost codes include demolition, framing, roofing, etc. |
| **Cost-Plus** | COST-PLUS is a method of invoicing customers based on the actual cost of producing the job plus an agreed-upon percentage markup to cover overhead and produce profit. While it is often used interchangeably with the term Time and Materials (T&M), it is not exactly the same since it includes a markup on a burdened labor rate instead of a specific billable hourly rate. See also T&M. |
| **CSI** | CSI is an acronym for Construction Standards Institute and typically refers to a list of cost breakdown codes developed by the Construction Standards Institute. |
| **Current Ratio** | CURRENT RATIO is one method of measuring the liquidity of a company. The formula = current assets ÷ current liabilities. The higher the number, the better positioned a company is to fully utilize its assets to pay for its liabilities. While a company should not have a current ratio less than 1, a ratio of 1.25 or higher is optimal. |
| **Depreciation Expense** | DEPRECIATION EXPENSE is the amount of depreciation that is included in the Profit and Loss Statement for the current year. When a company purchases an asset that will provide value for more than one year (such as equipment), it is capitalized on the Balance Sheet. The cost of the asset is charged off over time using the Depreciation Expense account. |
| **Direct Labor** | DIRECT LABOR is work performed by field personnel which is directly related to a specific job. These costs belong above the line. |
| **Equity** | EQUITY represents the net difference between the assets and the liabilities of a company. As an accounting term, it may not be equivalent to the net worth of a company. |

**Estimate**    ESTIMATE is an itemized listing of the amount of all expected hard costs for a job. All costs that will be charged to the job, above the line, are included in a job estimate. Overhead and profit should never be included in an estimate for job costing purposes.

**Expenses**    EXPENSES refer to company costs. In accounting software, expenses can be the name of a particular category of account. In QuickBooks all overhead accounts should be of the type "expense" and reflect overhead costs. See Below the Line.

**Fiscal Year**    FISCAL YEAR describes a business's accounting year. The period is usually twelve months which can begin during any month of the calendar year (e.g. April 1 to March 31). Many businesses use a calendar year (January 1 - December 31). Financial statements are typically produced based on a fiscal year, whereas job reports may be based on a different time frame.

**Fixed Price**    See Contract Price

**GAAP**    See Generally Accepted Accounting Practices

**General & Administrative (G&A)**    See Overhead

**Generally Accepted Accounting Principles**    GENERALLY ACCEPTED ACCOUNTING PRINCIPLES (GAAP) is a recognized common set of accounting principles, standards, and procedures. GAAP is a combination of accepted methods of doing accounting and policy board set authoritative standards.

**Gross Margin**    GROSS MARGIN is the gross profit shown as a percentage of sales.

**Gross Profit**    GROSS PROFIT is a dollar figure equal to revenue less COGS.

**Gross Profit Margin**    See Gross Margin

**Income Statement**    See Profit and Loss Statement

**Invoice**     INVOICE is a request for payment either from a vendor or subcontractor (a purchase invoice) or to a customer (a sales invoice). In QuickBooks, invoices refer specifically to sales invoices while purchase invoices are called bills.

**Item**     In QuickBooks, ITEMS are anything your company buys, sells, or resells in the course of business, such as products, shipping and handling charges, discounts, and sales tax (if applicable). Items are linked to accounts in the Chart of Accounts so that using an Item affects the general ledger. Items can be customized to automatically include descriptions. Items are the foundation of job cost reports and are found in the QuickBooks estimate, in cost-related transactions (bills, checks, credit card charges), in income-related transactions (invoices, sales receipts), and in job-related reports.

**Job Costing**     JOB COSTING is the process whereby costs are allocated to specific jobs. Costs above the line should be job costed while expenditures below the line are considered overhead and therefore not job specific.

**Job-related costs**     See Cost of Goods Sold, Above the line

**Lead carpenter** A lead carpenter is a highly skilled and experienced craftsman who is able to manage job sites with multiple carpenters and subcontractors.

**Lead carpenter system** In a lead carpenter system, the onsite responsibilities for running a job are handled by the lead carpenter who remains on site. The lead carpenter therefore deals with customers, solves onsite problems, orders materials, manages other production employees, and schedules and works with subcontractors.

**Liabilities**     LIABILITIES represent what a business owes. Accounts Payable, payroll liabilities, sales tax payable, lines of credit, and notes payable are all examples of liabilities. Typical categories include Short-term liabilities and Long-term liabilities based on when the liability is expected to be paid. Any liability that will be paid within the next twelve months is considered a short-term liability.

**Line of Credit**  LINE OF CREDIT is money borrowed from a bank to cover cash flow shortfalls. It is different from a loan in that the company draws against a maximum amount only as required and pays back principal when cash is available.

**Matching Principle**  MATCHING PRINCIPLE refers to the concept that the amount of income shown on a Profit and Loss Statement is related to the costs actually incurred. This means that if the COGS shows 25% of the expected costs of a job, the amount of revenue shown should be 25% of the total sales amount and the gross profit should be 25% of the total expected gross profit. Meaningful Profit and Loss Statements are prepared using the matching principle. It is also known as percentage of completion accounting and it can only be applied to accrual-based financials.

**Milestone Billing**  MILESTONE BILLING is a method of invoicing customers in which the total sales price of the job is broken down into specific phases. Each phase is invoiced either at the start of, or completion of each phase.

**Net Income**  NET INCOME is the dollar amount remaining from the total sales after all the expenses (COGS and Overhead) are subtracted. This amount is found both on the last line of the Profit and Loss Statement as well as the equity section of the Balance Sheet. For most small businesses, there is no distinction between Net Income and Net Profit.

**Net Margin**  See Net Profit Margin

**Net Profit**  See Net Income

**Net Profit Margin**  NET PROFIT MARGIN is the net profit shown as a percentage of sales.

**Other Income**  OTHER INCOME is income from activities that are earned as a result of the company's ordinary business. This could include interest income earned on savings accounts or gains on the sale of an asset (truck). Other income should not be included when calculating gross margin.

**Overbillings**  OVERBILLINGS is a liability account that represents the amount of revenue that has been invoiced but not earned, as determined using percentage of completion.

The opposite of Overbillings is Underbillings. Overbillings can also be referred to as Billings in Excess of Costs.

| | |
|---|---|
| **Overhead** | OVERHEAD costs are those costs required to run a company independent of production work. For example, the company must continue to pay for rent and utilities regardless of whether any jobs are in progress. See also General & Administrative, Below the line. |
| **P&L** | See Profit and Loss Statement |
| **Payroll Burden** | PAYROLL BURDEN represents the additional costs (above and beyond gross wages) required to compensate and support an employee in the field. It includes payroll taxes, workers' compensation, liability insurance, and other company-paid perks and benefits. In construction it is not unusual for the burden to be close to (or even exceed) the hourly wage amount, especially when the company offers a generous benefit package. |
| **Payroll Liabilities** | PAYROLL LIABILITIES are accumulated as a result of paying wages to employees. Payroll Liabilities consist of dollars withheld from the employee (such as federal and state income taxes and FICA) as well as company paid taxes (such as matching FICA and FUTA). In QuickBooks, payroll liabilities are paid through a special function called Pay Liabilities. |
| **Percentage of Completion Accounting** | See Matching Principle |
| **Percentage of Completion Invoicing** | See Progress Billing |
| **Prepaid Expenses** | PREPAID EXPENSES is an Asset account that represents the amount of money paid in advance of receiving goods or services. Typically, insurance premiums are paid in advance of the coverage contained in the policy. For example, you may pay for liability insurance on a quarterly basis. If you pay on July 1 for coverage for July, August, and September, then ⅓ of the payment would be considered an expense (for July) and appear on the Profit and Loss Statement. The remaining ⅔ would be considered prepaid and should appear on your Balance Sheet as an Asset. In each subsequent month, another third of the expense should be reclassified to the Profit and Loss Statement and removed from the Balance Sheet. |

**Production Employees**  PRODUCTION EMPLOYEES perform production labor on specific customer jobs.

**Profit and Loss Statement**  PROFIT AND LOSS STATEMENT shows revenue and expenses for a specific period of time. A key element of this statement, and one that distinguishes it from a balance sheet, is that the amounts shown on the statement represent transactions over a period of time while the items represented on the Balance Sheet show information as of a specific date (or point in time). It is also known as the Income Statement.

**Progress Billing**  PROGRESS BILLING is a method of invoicing customers in which the total sales price of the job is broken down into specific phases. The invoice is prepared including the percentage of each phase completed at the time of invoicing. Progress Billing is also referred to as AIA invoicing or percentage of completion invoicing.

**Retained Earnings**  RETAINED EARNINGS are profits that a business has earned since inception, less any money paid as draws, distributions, or dividends. Retained Earnings appears on the Balance Sheet in the equity section.

**Revenue Recognition**  REVENUE RECOGNITION is the issue of when revenue appears on the Profit and Loss Statement.

**T&M**  T&M is a method of invoicing customers in which a markup percentage is applied to the actual costs of the materials and subcontractors, and labor is charged at a predetermined hourly rate. While it is often used interchangeably with the term Cost Plus, it is not exactly the same since it uses a specific billable hourly rate rather than applying an across-the-board markup to actual costs including labor. See also Cost Plus.

**Trial Balance**  TRIAL BALANCE is a listing of all of the accounts in the general ledger and their balances as of a specified date.

**Underbillings**  UNDERBILLINGS is an asset account that represents the amount of earned revenue that has yet to be invoiced as determined, using percentage of completion.

The opposite of Underbillings is Overbillings. Underbillings can also be referred to as Costs in Excess of Billings.

**Variance**      VARIANCE is the difference between a projected number and the actual number. In construction, variance usually refers to the discrepancy between budgeted and actual costs on a project.

**WIP Adjustment**      WIP ADJUSTMENT adjusts the income on the Profit and Loss Statement to bring it into alignment with actual costs. Income and costs on jobs are "matched" (see Matching Principle) based on the percent complete to show actual profit and accurate margin. Many contractors who sell projects at a fixed contract price will front load invoices. If the total amount invoiced is considered income, the company appears to be more profitable than it really is. After the bulk of the customer's money is invoiced, the contractor may continue to incur significant costs, at which point the company appears to be less profitable. This fluctuation in profit is due to a timing difference on invoicing, not on true profitability. Therefore, a WIP adjustment will smooth out this fluctuation.

# APPENDIX B – SELECTED KEY CONCEPTS

This appendix contains a reprint of selected key figures from the book. It can be used as a quick reference guide. For more detailed explanation of each concept, refer to the original chapter text.

| Sales price | - | Job Costs | = | Gross Profit |
|---|---|---|---|---|
| $42,000 | | $31,000 | | $11,000 |
| | | | | |
| Gross Profit | ÷ | Sales price | = | Gross Margin |
| $11,000 | | $42,000 | | 26% |

**Figure 2-1. To determine gross profit, subtract job costs from the sales price. To determine gross margin, divide gross profit in dollars by the sale price of the job.**

| Gross Profit | - | Job's share of overhead | = | Net Profit |
|---|---|---|---|---|
| $11,000 | | $8,000 | | $3,000 |
| | | | | |
| Net profit | ÷ | Selling price | = | Net Profit Margin |
| $3,000 | | $42,000 | | 7% |

**Figure 2-2. To determine net profit, subtract overhead costs from gross profit. To determine net profit margin, divide the net profit in dollars by the selling price.**

| | | Margin |
|---|---|---|
| Income | $42,000 | |
| Cost of Goods Sold | -$31,000 | |
| Gross Profit | $11,000 | 26% |
| | | |
| Overhead | -$8,000 | |
| Net Profit | $3,000 | 7% |

**Figure 2-3. Sample job as displayed in a P&L**

| Overhead | ÷ Total Sales | = Overhead as % of sales |
|---|---|---|
| $194,531 | $800,000 | 24.4% |

Figure 3-3. When overhead costs are separated from job costs, they can be expressed as a percentage of sales.

| Total Sales | $800,000 |
|---|---|
| Total Cost of Goods Sold | -$686,257 |
| Gross Profit | $113,743 |
| Gross Profit Margin | 14.2% |

Figure 3-4. Gross Margin shows, as a percentage, how much remains after job costs have been deducted from total sales dollars.

| Construction Revenue | $800,000 |
|---|---|
| Total Overhead Expenses | $194,531 |
| Overhead as % of Income | 24.4% |

Figure 3-5. Expressing overhead costs as a percentage of total sales allows comparison with Gross Profit Margin.

| Markup in $ | ÷ Sales Price | = Margin |
|---|---|---|
| $100 | $300 | 33.3% |

Figure 4-5. Margin is calculated by dividing the markup in dollars by the sales price of the job.

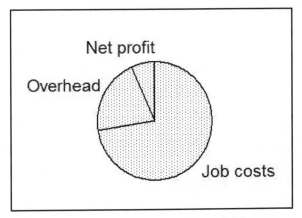

**Figure 4-9. Total sales will always be the sum of job costs + overhead + profit.**

| Gross Profit | ÷ Margin | = Sales Volume |
|:---:|:---:|:---:|
| $259,000 | 21% | $1,233,333 |

**Figure 4-14. To determine a target sales volume ($), divide gross profit by the estimated margin (%).**

| Gross Profit | ÷ Margin | = Sales Volume |
|:---:|:---:|:---:|
| $259,000 | 32% | $809,375 |

**Figure 4-15. Target sales volume will decrease as estimated gross margin increases.**

| Sales Price | - Job Costs | = Gross Profit | ÷ Sales Price | = Gross Margin |
|:---:|:---:|:---:|:---:|:---:|
| $110,000 | $85,600 | $24,400 | $110,000 | 22% |

**Figure 5-2. Sample job margin calculation.**

```
Income
Total Income                      $    1,300,000

Cost of Goods Sold
Labor Costs                            $300,000
Materials Costs                        $240,000
Subcontractor Costs                    $250,000
Equipment Rental Costs                  $37,500
Other Direct Costs                      $12,500
Total COGS                             $840,000


Gross Profit ($)                       $460,000

Overhead Expenses
Advertising                             $26,000
Office Supplies                          $6,500
Postage                                  $1,500
Rent                                    $18,000
Utilities                                $6,500
```

**Figure 6-1. "The Line" in a fictional P&L.**

```
Income
Labor Income                    $      400,000
Materials Income                $      400,000
Subcontractor Income            $      400,000
Equipment Rental Income         $       75,000
Other Direct Income             $       25,000
Total Income                    $    1,300,000

Cost of Goods Sold
Labor Costs                     $      300,000
Materials Costs                 $      240,000
Subcontractor Costs             $      250,000
Equipment Rental Costs          $       37,500
Other Direct Costs              $       12,500
Total COGS                      $      840,000

Gross Profit ($)                $      460,000
Gross Margin (%)                        35.38%
```

**Figure 6-2. Chart of Accounts with parallelism between income and COGS accounts.**

# APPENDIX C – MARKUP TO MARGIN CONVERSION TABLE

## Markup to Margin Conversion Table

| Markup | Margin | Markup | Margin | Markup | Margin |
|--------|--------|--------|--------|--------|--------|
| 1.00% | 0.99% | 51.00% | 33.77% | 101.00% | 50.25% |
| 2.00% | 1.96% | 52.00% | 34.21% | 102.00% | 50.50% |
| 3.00% | 2.91% | 53.00% | 34.64% | 103.00% | 50.74% |
| 4.00% | 3.85% | 54.00% | 35.06% | 104.00% | 50.98% |
| 5.00% | 4.76% | 55.00% | 35.48% | 105.00% | 51.22% |
| 6.00% | 5.66% | 56.00% | 35.90% | 106.00% | 51.46% |
| 7.00% | 6.54% | 57.00% | 36.31% | 107.00% | 51.69% |
| 8.00% | 7.41% | 58.00% | 36.71% | 108.00% | 51.92% |
| 9.00% | 8.26% | 59.00% | 37.11% | 109.00% | 52.15% |
| 10.00% | 9.09% | 60.00% | 37.50% | 110.00% | 52.38% |
| 11.00% | 9.91% | 61.00% | 37.89% | 111.00% | 52.61% |
| 12.00% | 10.71% | 62.00% | 38.27% | 112.00% | 52.83% |
| 13.00% | 11.50% | 63.00% | 38.65% | 113.00% | 53.05% |
| 14.00% | 12.28% | 64.00% | 39.02% | 114.00% | 53.27% |
| 15.00% | 13.04% | 65.00% | 39.39% | 115.00% | 53.49% |
| 16.00% | 13.79% | 66.00% | 39.76% | 116.00% | 53.70% |
| 17.00% | 14.53% | 67.00% | 40.12% | 117.00% | 53.92% |
| 18.00% | 15.25% | 68.00% | 40.48% | 118.00% | 54.13% |
| 19.00% | 15.97% | 69.00% | 40.83% | 119.00% | 54.34% |
| 20.00% | 16.67% | 70.00% | 41.18% | 120.00% | 54.55% |
| 21.00% | 17.36% | 71.00% | 41.52% | 121.00% | 54.75% |
| 22.00% | 18.03% | 72.00% | 41.86% | 122.00% | 54.95% |
| 23.00% | 18.70% | 73.00% | 42.20% | 123.00% | 55.16% |
| 24.00% | 19.35% | 74.00% | 42.53% | 124.00% | 55.36% |
| 25.00% | 20.00% | 75.00% | 42.86% | 125.00% | 55.56% |
| 26.00% | 20.63% | 76.00% | 43.18% | 126.00% | 55.75% |
| 27.00% | 21.26% | 77.00% | 43.50% | 127.00% | 55.95% |
| 28.00% | 21.88% | 78.00% | 43.82% | 128.00% | 56.14% |
| 29.00% | 22.48% | 79.00% | 44.13% | 129.00% | 56.33% |
| 30.00% | 23.08% | 80.00% | 44.44% | 130.00% | 56.52% |
| 31.00% | 23.66% | 81.00% | 44.75% | 131.00% | 56.71% |
| 32.00% | 24.24% | 82.00% | 45.05% | 132.00% | 56.90% |
| 33.00% | 24.81% | 83.00% | 45.36% | 133.00% | 57.08% |
| 34.00% | 25.37% | 84.00% | 45.65% | 134.00% | 57.26% |
| 35.00% | 25.93% | 85.00% | 45.95% | 135.00% | 57.45% |
| 36.00% | 26.47% | 86.00% | 46.24% | 136.00% | 57.63% |
| 37.00% | 27.01% | 87.00% | 46.52% | 137.00% | 57.81% |
| 38.00% | 27.54% | 88.00% | 46.81% | 138.00% | 57.98% |
| 39.00% | 28.06% | 89.00% | 47.09% | 139.00% | 58.16% |
| 40.00% | 28.57% | 90.00% | 47.37% | 140.00% | 58.33% |
| 41.00% | 29.08% | 91.00% | 47.64% | 141.00% | 58.51% |
| 42.00% | 29.58% | 92.00% | 47.92% | 142.00% | 58.68% |
| 43.00% | 30.07% | 93.00% | 48.19% | 143.00% | 58.85% |
| 44.00% | 30.56% | 94.00% | 48.45% | 144.00% | 59.02% |
| 45.00% | 31.03% | 95.00% | 48.72% | 145.00% | 59.18% |
| 46.00% | 31.51% | 96.00% | 48.98% | 146.00% | 59.35% |
| 47.00% | 31.97% | 97.00% | 49.24% | 147.00% | 59.51% |
| 48.00% | 32.43% | 98.00% | 49.49% | 148.00% | 59.68% |
| 49.00% | 32.89% | 99.00% | 49.75% | 149.00% | 59.84% |
| 50.00% | 33.33% | 100.00% | 50.00% | 150.00% | 60.00% |

**What's YOUR target?**
And what are you achieving?

## APPENDIX D – RESOURCES

The authors believe that the most successful contractors are those who constantly strive to improve themselves and their companies. Improving means changing, and change relies on getting different ideas on how to do things. In construction this can – and should – mean researching new products, materials, and methods. Too often this research is limited to the production side of things. We suggest that readers spend similar effort looking into new products (technology or software), materials (professional journals, books on business and management, etc.), and methods (sales training, leadership workshops, etc.) related to the business side of things.

There are many books, publications, and organizations out there, easily researched via the Internet. Here is a sample of the resources out there:

### Professional Organizations

**National Association of Home Builders (NAHB)**
1201 15th Street, NW
Washington, DC 20005
800-368-5242
202-266-8200 x0
Fax 202-266-8400
www.nahb.org

**National Association of the Remodeling Industry (NARI)**
780 Lee Street
Suite 200
Des Plaines, IL 60016
800-611-NARI (6274)
847-298-9200
Fax 847-298-9225
www.nari.org
E-mail: info@nari.org

**National Association of Women in Construction (NAWIC)**
327 S. Adams St.
Fort Worth, TX 76104
800-552-3506
817-877-5551
Fax 817-877-0324
www.nawic.org
Email: nawic@nawic.org

## Professional Publications (several offer free subscriptions)

*Builder Magazine*
*Building Design & Construction Magazine*
*Coastal Contractor*
*Constructech*
*Essential Kitchen & Bathroom Business*
*Journal of Construction Engineering and Management*
*The Journal of Light Construction*
*Professional Builder*
*Professional Remodeler*
*Qualified Remodeler*
*Remodeling*
*Replacement Contractor*
*Restoration & Remediation*
*Tools of the Trade*

## Conferences & Shows

Remodeling Show
JLC Live
International Builders Show
World of Concrete
State and regional builders' shows – check online

## Construction Business Management

*The E Myth Contractor*
    – Michael E. Gerber, Published by HarperBusiness
*Lead Carpenter Handbook: The Complete Hands On Guide To Successful*
*Job Site Management*
    –Tim Faller, Published by Journal of Light Construction
Bookstore (National Association of Home Builders):
www.nahbrc.com/bookstore
Builder Books: www.builderbooks.com
Craftsman Book Company: www.craftsman-book.com
JLC Online Bookstore: www.jlconline.com and click link to bookstore

## Sales Resources

*If I Sell You I Have a Job. If I Serve You I Create A Career!*
    – Michael S. Gorman, Published by TechKnowledge
Sandler Training: www.sandler.com

# About the Authors

Melanie Hodgdon (Business Systems Management, Inc.) and Leslie Shiner, MBA (The ShinerGroup) both manage successful consulting and coaching companies. With over 40 years combined experience, they help contractors better understand and improve business practices and maximize profits. In 2007, they began to work on a series of joint projects that would capitalize on their combined talents. This book is one product of that collaboration. They can be reached via e-mail.

*L_Shiner@ShinerGroup.com*

*Melanie@bsm-inc.org*

===============================

Since 1994, Melanie Hodgdon has worked with clients to identify financial and procedural challenges and generate realistic solutions that reflect the resources and style of their companies. With a background in teaching, construction, and computerized accounting, she has made the construction industry her specialty area. Melanie writes for various construction industry magazines, speaks on business and QuickBooks topics at construction shows, records training webinars for a variety of organizations, and is a Certified QuickBooks ProAdvisor.

Her ideal client is a small- to mid-sized company owner who has either recently hung up his toolbelt or has been awakened to the need to be more of a businessman and less of a hands-on contractor. Melanie blends logic and insight to create company-specific solutions to help contractors operate more profitably.

She currently lives in Bristol, Maine with Ed, her husband of 35-plus years, where they have been remodeling their ever-growing house since purchasing it in 1980. She claims it should be done any day now.

===============================

Leslie Shiner has more than 25 years of experience working as a financial and management consultant for the construction industry. As an author, trainer and speaker, she has wowed audiences with her humor and simple-to-understand explanations of how to run your company by the numbers.

Leslie's postgraduate education focused on finance and accounting, culminating in an MBA from UC Berkeley. In addition to being a Certified QuickBooks ProAdvisor and Sage Certified Consultant, she has been a Master Builder master trainer since 1998. She is a regular contributor to several industry magazines, produces recorded and live webinars, and teaches around the country at industry events. Her passion for the numbers has always helped her clients become financially savvy business owners.

She currently lives in Mill Valley, California, and is very proud of her family, including her husband Dan, children Rachel, Zachary, and Netiya, not to mention two cats and a dog. As a self-diagnosed workaholic, she continues to struggle with work-life balance, just like Mike!

==============================

Made in the USA
Middletown, DE
12 January 2022

58504893R00130